THE

Miriam Stoppard

HEALTH AND BEAUTY

BOOK

THE
HEALTH AND BEAUTY
BOOK

DORLING KINDERSLEY
LONDON

For Beverly, Gwyn, Petrina and Val

Editor Ricki Ostrov
Art Editor Sally Powell
Designer Sally Hibbard

Editorial Director Amy Carroll
Art Director Denise Brown

First published in Great Britain in 1988 by
Dorling Kindersley Publishers Limited,
9 Henrietta Street, London WC2E 8PS

Copyright © 1988
Dorling Kindersley Limited, London

All rights reserved. No part of this publication may be reproduced, stored in a retrieval system, or transmitted in any form or by any means, electronic, mechanical, photocopying, recording or otherwise, without the prior written permission of the copyright owner.

British Library Cataloguing in Publication Data
Stoppard, Miriam
 Miriam Stoppard's Health and Beauty Book
 1. Beauty, personal
 I . Title
 646.7'2 RA778
ISBN 0–86318–299–2 (hardback)
     0–86318–296–8 (paperback)

Typeset by Dataset, St. Clements, Oxford

Reproduction by Hong Kong Graphic Arts Limited

Printed in Italy by Graphicom Srl

CONTENTS

FOREWORD

I undertook this book firmly convinced of the following. In terms of health and appearance, we can all make more of ourselves; we only need to find the time and make the effort; the effort is worth it. Though radical changes are impossible — no one can halt ageing — we can all make the best of ourselves. Indeed, we owe it to ourselves to capitalize on our good points. It's not frivolous, it's not arrogant, and it's not a waste of time. It's good for us. The benefits are unquestioned in terms of well-being, morale, and, eventually, happiness.

It's easy to neglect yourself if you have the idea that health and beauty routines are the province only of women with money and leisure. Well, that need not be so. Paying attention to your appearance need not be expensive. I'm personally very much against high-priced cosmetics boasting unproven claims that are impossible to deliver and couched in pseudo-scientific terms. The cost of such cosmetics is not to cover the exotic sounding ingredients, it is to cover expensive advertising campaigns and packaging. As to the ingredients — however persuasive the selling line sounds do not believe a word of it; the cheapest version is usually as effective as the most costly.

Caring for yourself need not be time-consuming, either, and every woman could do with a few tips on routines that can be fitted in between other things. They're all here and worth trying. It only takes 10 minutes for my skin care routine, or 25 minutes to wash and blow dry hair; perfect nails only need 60 minutes once a week.

Give yourself a slightly higher priority than you ever have before. Find the time and make the effort. You're worth it.

HEALTHY
LIVING

HEALTHY LIVING

It is difficult to be either healthy or beautiful if you neglect yourself. This doesn't just mean caring for your external appearance, such as wearing makeup or having a flattering hairstyle. It also means maintaining the health of your inner self, including paying attention to the foods you eat, getting regular exercise, limiting smoking and drinking, and trying to eliminate some of the stress in your life. All of these affect the way that you look and feel.

Good health is not just the absence of illness, it is also feeling good about yourself so that you can live life to the fullest and achieve your true potential. To accomplish this you may need to make either major or minor changes to your lifestyle, and so increase your satisfaction with life, improve your mental and physical well-being, and allow yourself to feel and look better. Maintaining your health can give you a zest for life and the energy, determination, and ability to achieve your goals.

EATING FOR HEALTH

It is no secret that what we eat affects the way we look and feel, and that food is essential for a healthy life. Food is the fuel the body uses to give us energy and keep our bodies functioning efficiently. It also provides the building blocks for the growth and repair of tissues.

Know your nutrients

The main nutrients that must be included in the daily diet are proteins, carbohydrates, fats, fibre, and salt. In addition, a certain amount of vitamins and minerals are needed for the body to function efficiently.

Protein is vital for the growth, repair and replacement of tissues. It can be found in large quantities in animal products, such as meat, poultry, and dairy products, and in smaller quantities in fruits and vegetables, cereals and grains.

Carbohydrates provide energy for the body. They are found in starches and sugars. Not all carbohydrates are the same in terms of health; refined, or sugary, carbohydrates should be avoided while the amount of complex, or starchy, carbohydrates should be increased in most people's diet.

Fat, which is the highest energy food, provides fatty acids that are essential to the body's metabolism, but some fats are better than others. A healthy diet should be low in saturated fats, which are primarily found in red meat and dairy products. Monounsaturated fats, have little effect on the health while polyunsaturated fats appear to have a beneficial effect.

Fibre is important because it aids proper digestion and bowel action and may reduce the tendency to intestinal and bowel disorders. All dietary fibre comes from plant products, such as fruits and vegetables, cereals and grains; it is not found in animal or dairy products.

Salt, or sodium, is essential to life to regulate body fluids. The average person eats about 10 times more than is necessary, and too much salt can lead to high blood pressure in certain people.

Vitamins are chemicals that help regulate metabolism and convert carbohydrates and fat into energy. The body can store excess amounts of some vitamins but others, such as vitamin C, are not stored in the body and must be replaced daily. Minerals are essential for regulating body fluids and the balance of chemicals within the body. They are found in both plant and animal products. Both vitamins and minerals are found in a wide variety of foods, and if you eat a well-balanced diet you should not need any supplements.

Proteins

Proteins are needed for the growth, repair and replacement of body tissues. They are found in pulses and cereals as well as in meat, fish and in dairy products. Try to avoid eating too much beef, lamb, and pork, which have high fat contents. Instead eat fish, poultry, and vegetable protein sources such as nuts and grains.

Carbohydrates

Carbohydrates are a major source of energy but eaten in excess they are stored in the body as fat. They are available as natural sugars and starches present in cereals, grains and root vegetables. Eat unrefined products such as wholemeal bread and brown rice, and green and yellow vegetables and potatoes.

Fats

Fats are a concentrated source of energy that provide more calories than any other food. Saturated fats are found mainly in animal products, dairy products and eggs. Monounsaturated fats are most commonly found in poultry, margarine and olive oil. Polyunsaturated fats are found in fish, corn and safflower oil.

Fibre

Fibre is the indigestible residue of plant products that passes through the digestive system unabsorbed. While fibre contains no energy value or nutrients it is important for a healthy bowel action and adds bulk to the faeces. It is also thought to help protect against some forms of heart disease.

A balanced diet

There has been much discussion and debate about the balance of protein, fats and carbohydrates that is needed for a healthy diet. It is now thought that 60 percent of your daily calories should be obtained from complex carbohydrates (those from starches rather than sugars), another 20–25 percent of your calories should be obtained from fats, and 15–20 percent of your total daily calorie intake from proteins.

Most foods provide more than one nutrient, so eating a varied diet will ensure that you get all that you need. An easy way to plan a balanced diet is to use the basic four food groups as a sort of menu. You should choose 2 or 3 servings of protein (lean meat, poultry, fish, eggs and dried beans and peas); 2 servings of dairy products (milk, cheese and yoghurt); 4 servings of fruit and vegetables; and 4 servings of bread, grain, pasta, rice, or cereal.

Healthy cooking

It is not just the foods you eat but also the way that you prepare them that makes for a healthy diet. When cooking you should try to:

- Bake, broil or steam food rather than frying.
- Stir-fry foods or, when frying, use as little oil and fat as possible and use polyunsaturated fat.
- Use non-stick cookware, which cuts down on the amount of fat you need to use.
- Use salt sparingly; try using herbs and spices to add flavour rather than salt.
- Cook vegetables and fruits with their skin to retain the fibre.
- Steam rather than boil vegetables, as vitamins and minerals are lost in the cooking water.

THE EFFECTS OF SMOKING

Cigarette smoking is one of the worst habits you can possibly have if you truly care about the way you look and feel. Every cigarette you smoke may shorten your life by about five and a half minutes. Smoking is the major cause of illness and premature death in the Western world; it is estimated that nearly 30,000 women die because of smoking every year. And yet more and more women are taking up smoking and are less successful than men at giving up.

Risks of smoking

Cigarettes are a proven factor in the development of lung cancer. They also cause cancers of the mouth, throat, and gullet, and there may be a connection between cigarette smoking and the development of cervical cancer. Smoking causes chronic lung diseases such as emphysema, and increases the risk of stroke and heart attacks by inhibiting circulation, which leads to the development of cholesterol deposits in artery walls. Women who smoke and use the contraceptive pill have a greater risk of developing heart disease. Smoking may also affect fertility and bring on early menopause, while pregnant women who smoke during their pregnancy increase the risk of having low birthweight babies.

In addition to the internal effects of smoking, it also affects how you look. Smoking makes the skin age faster and wrinkle earlier, and affects the tone and texture of the skin. In addition, it is one of the major causes of bad breath, and can cause tooth and gum decay. The nicotine in cigarettes also stains the teeth and fingernails.

Giving up

Nobody can pretend that quitting is easy, but the sooner you stop the healthier you will immediately become. Although many of the cigarette-related diseases are fatal, if you have not smoked for more than 10 years your chances of contracting those diseases are no greater than someone who has never smoked.

If you truly want to give up, the best way is to stop completely. It takes real willpower and determination as habits are hard to break. It takes at least six to eight weeks to stop feeling the need and craving for a cigarette, and about a year before you can really say that you are a non-smoker. If you feel that you cannot give up smoking on your own, there is plenty of help and support available. Nicotine chewing gum may help to relieve the cravings; an antismoking group or clinic will give you moral support; and hypnotherapy or acupuncture works for some people to relieve withdrawal symptoms.

THE EFFECTS OF ALCOHOL

Drinking in moderation is probably not harmful, but alcohol is an addictive drug and you can easily become dependent on it. Although we often think of alcohol as a stimulant it, in fact, acts as a tranquillizer and depressant, dulling our brain and nervous systems. In small quantities this can produce a pleasantly relaxed feeling, but in larger amounts this can lead to gross impairment of memory, judgement, coordination and emotional reactions. After a heavy drinking session you are likely to feel tired, nauseated, and may have a headache as a result of the damaging effect of alcohol on the stomach and intestines.

Regular consumption of even small amounts of alcohol may cause social and family problems. Large amounts severely damage health. Brain shrinkage may occur in even moderate drinkers. Obesity is likely as a result of the high energy value of most alcoholic drinks, and liver damage occurs so that the body can no longer process nutrients or medication.

Excessive alcohol consumption has special dangers for women. Because our bodies contain less water than men's, alcohol has a greater toxic effect on our

ALCOHOL CONSUMPTION

Women should aim to keep their alcohol consumption well below 30gm a day. This amount is the equivalent of 3 small glasses of beer, 3 small glasses of wine, or 3 small measures of spirits.

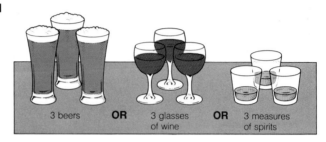

3 beers **OR** 3 glasses of wine **OR** 3 measures of spirits

body organs. Women are more susceptible than men to the harmful effects of alcohol on the liver because of the differences in the way their livers process alcohol. And, apart from endangering their own health, women who drink during pregnancy risk damaging their unborn baby, which may be born underweight and mentally retarded.

If you feel that your drinking is getting out of control or that you are becoming dependent on alcohol, consult your doctor who may be able to advise you or refer you to a counselling organization.

GETTING FIT

Feeling fit and healthy is one of the goals all of us want to achieve, and exercise plays an important part. Regular exercise makes you feel good, both physically and mentally. In addition, exercise is the ideal partner for dieting if you are trying to lose weight. It will increase the rate at which you lose, ensure that what you lose is fat and not muscle tissue, and help your body tone up while it is changing shape; it also suppresses appetite.

There are additional benefits to be gained from regular exercise. It can help you to better cope with tension and stress, improve your posture and circulation, and ward off some of the effects of ageing. It can also help you to sleep better, feel more relaxed, improve your concentration, and provide all round better health. And, of course, you will look better.

Types of exercise

Different types of exercise help the body in different ways (see chart page 16). Some help to maintain mobility so that the body is limber and can stretch easily. Others make the body stronger, not only strengthening the muscles but also the bones and joints. Aerobic exercise, which is the most beneficial, is that which conditions the heart and lungs to better cope with the body's need for extra oxygen, and may help protect against heart disease in later years. Aerobic exercise is also the kind that aids weight loss. Many exercises combine some degree of all three types of fitness, and you should decide on one that is right for you.

THE BENEFITS OF EXERCISE

Heart, lungs and arteries Regular, vigorous activity will increase the strength and resiliency of the heart and lungs, helping them to become more efficient and less prone to disease. Exercise may also decrease blood pressure, thereby reducing the risk of hardening of the arteries. At the same time exercise may widen the arteries and make a complete blockage, by a clot for instance, less likely.

Joints that are regularly exercised will maintain their strength and flexibility. Under-use contributes to stiffening and weakness of the ligaments that support and protect the joints.

Muscles Exercise increases muscle tone, thereby conditioning the entire body. Because the muscles that move the legs are among the largest in the body, activities that use the legs, such as swimming, running or cycling, are excellent ways to place healthy demands on the heart and lungs.

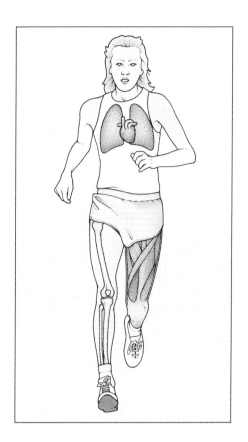

Choosing an exercise

Your age and health play an important part in the type of exercise you need, but you must choose one that you enjoy doing and one that fits in with your lifestyle. How often you exercise is important, because the real benefits of exercise only result from activity that is performed at least three times a week; aerobic exercise must be done continuously for at least 20 minutes at a time.

Some people go running because, except for special shoes, it is free and can be done almost anywhere. Others have a pool near them and swimming comes easily. If you have a gym or fitness centre near you, you may be able to take a couple of dance or aerobics classes to see if the routine suits you. Many people prefer solitary exercise, using the time to get in touch with themselves, while others enjoy the social atmosphere of a dance or exercise class. You may want to try different forms of exercise to see which suits you best.

In addition to your regular exercise program, you should try to fit in some daily exercise, such as walking the dog, getting off the bus a stop or two earlier and walking to work or home. This will also provide some benefits, and help to make exercise a regular part of your life.

WARM UP ROUTINE

You should always spend a few minutes warming up and stretching your muscles before you exercise, as cold muscles are easily injured. Always perform these stretches on a non-slip surface unless otherwise instructed. Never force your body into a stretch, and do not hold your breath, as this causes tension.

Take feet 3 feet apart, knees straight, arms out to side. Keep spine extended, chest open. Stretch sideways only, not forwards.

Do not try to go down too far. Hold for 30 seconds each side.

Take feet wide apart, with toes pointing forwards and arches of your feet lifted up. Turn thighs outwards, knees straight. Breathing out, stretch arms straight above head. Take a few deep breaths, stretching up as you breathe out.

Then bring arms down to shoulder level and stretch arms out strongly from spine into your fingertips. Hold for a few seconds, then repeat the entire sequence twice.

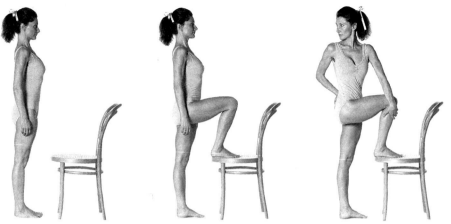

Place chair so it cannot slip. Face chair, put one foot on chair seat with thigh parallel with floor. Twist around, stretch up. Open chest, relax shoulders. Hold for 30 seconds, then repeat other side.

Lie on your front on a rug or blanket with arms down by side and palms of hands facing ceiling. Lift legs and shoulders off floor. Lengthen spine, open chest, stretch back of neck. Do not take head higher than the feet. Hold for a few seconds, repeat twice.

Kneel on a rug or blanket on the floor, sitting on your heels. Link fingers together, turn palms outwards and stretch arms up over your head. Release your fingers. Keep your bottom down on your heels. Then bring your arms down close to your thighs and fold your body forwards. Lower your head until it touches the ground. Breathe out as you bend forwards and breathe naturally for about a minute. Then breathe in and come up. Repeat the stretch, again starting with your fingers linked, the opposite thumb on top.

The following chart is a rough guide to the fitness benefits of various sports. One bullet indicates minimal benefits in that category, two bullets means good benefits, and three bullets indicates excellent benefits.

FITNESS BENEFITS OF VARIOUS ACTIVITIES

Activity	Aerobic fitness	Strength	Flexibility
Archery	•	•	••
Badminton	••	••	••
Basketball	••	••	••
Bowls/Bowling	•	•	•
Boxing	••	•••	••
Canoeing	••	•••	••
Cricket	•	••	••
Cycling	•••	•••	••
Dancing	••	•••	••
Fencing	•	•••	•••
Football	••	•••	••
Golf	•	•	••
Gymnastics	•	•••	•••
Hockey (field)	••	••	••
Hockey (ice)	••	••	••
Jogging/Running	•••	•••	•
Judo/Karate	•	••	•••
Lacrosse	••	•••	••
Riding (horse)	•	••	•
Rowing	•••	•••	•
Rugby	••	•••	•
Sailing	•	••	•
Skating (ice)	••	••	••
Skating (roller)	••	••	••
Skiing (cross country)	•••	•••	••
Skiing (downhill)	••	•••	••
Skipping rope	•••	•	•
Squash	••	••	••
Swimming	•••	•••	•••
Tennis	••	•••	••
Volleyball	••	•••	••
Walking (brisk)	••	•	•
Waterskiing	•	•••	•
Weight training	•	•••	••
Yoga	•	••	•••

Getting started

If you have not exercised for a long time, or if you have any physical problems, it is wise to discuss your plans with your doctor. Once you are ready, never exercise on a full stomach; you should allow at least an hour after eating to give the food a chance to settle. Always warm up before starting to exercise. Most classes have a warm up period, but if you are exercising on your own, spend about five minutes limbering up and doing mild stretches to warm your muscles.

You must be prepared to spend time and energy on your exercise program. How often you exercise is important; aim for three to four times a week until you have reached your level of fitness. And don't get discouraged; the more out of shape you are when you start, the longer it will take you to work up to your fitness level. But you will start to notice the benefits earlier than someone who is already fit.

DEVELOPING GOOD POSTURE

Your posture, which includes how you stand, walk and sit, can make a great difference to how you look and feel. Good posture means that you use the minimum amount of energy and effort to balance your body correctly, and you put less strain on the muscles, bones and joints. Bad posture is tiring and wastes a great deal of energy. Your muscles will be stretched and pulled to cope with the body's unnatural movements, which can lead to tension, joint damage, pain or discomfort.

You will feel the benefits of good posture immediately. You will look slimmer, your muscles and joints will be under less strain, your lungs can expand and work more efficiently, as can your digestive tract. Remember too, that just as your mood can affect your posture, that your posture can affect your mood.

Practising good posture

In addition to standing correctly, it is important to maintain good posture when moving or sitting. If you are carrying bags of shopping, try to balance the weight equally; don't carry all your packages on one side of the body, which puts excessive strain on that side and throws your hips out of alignment.

When sitting, choose a chair that supports your back and the whole of your thighs, and allows both feet to rest evenly on the floor. This will help prevent you from developing a rounded spine and will also put less strain on your back. Try not to cross your legs as this inhibits circulation.

If you are sitting at a desk or table with work in front of you, try not to bring your head forwards, which causes strain on the neck and back. Instead, bring your hands forward to your work while keeping the back upright.

CHECKING POSTURE

It is a good idea to check your posture occasionally to see if you are standing correctly. You can do this yourself or have a friend check it with a pole. In either method, when you are standing correctly there should be a little gap between the door or pole and the back of your body at the waist and the back of the neck.

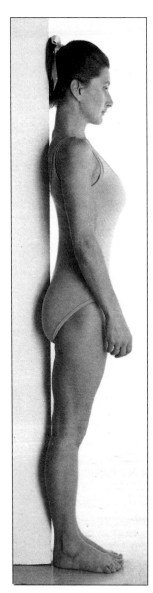

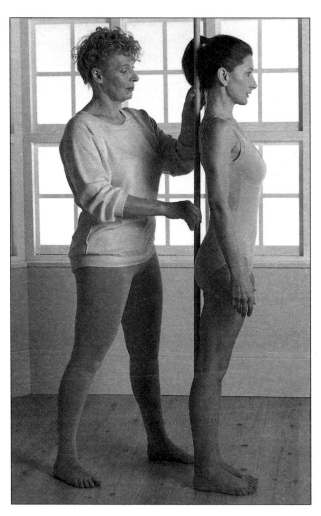

To check your posture yourself, stand against a wall or door and look in a mirror (left). To check your posture with a pole (above), the pole should be placed behind you so that its base just touches the back of your heels, your lower back, the back of your chest and the back of your head.

You should learn to use your body correctly when lifting or carrying heavy weights. This will protect your bones, muscles and joints from strain, sprain and even tears. When lifting a heavy object, bend your knees and let the resilient muscles of the legs take the strain, not the back. Hold the weight close to your body, tuck in your pelvis to minimize stress on the spine, and never bend down from the waist.

When bending down to pick something off the floor, prevent straining by kneeling instead of stooping. If you are moving heavy objects, lean your back against the object and push it away with your back and legs. Never push the object away from you with your arms and chest.

STRESS

Stress is one of the most common problems affecting women today, and can affect you at any stage in your life. Pressures and emotional upheavals are part of all our lives, but their mental and physical effects vary from person to person. A moderate amount of stress can be good for you, as it can improve performance, efficiency and productivity. But too much stress, especially continuing over a period of time, can cause a wide variety of physical and emotional disorders. You need to learn to recognize which situations are most stressful for you and find effective ways of dealing with them to avoid the adverse effects of too much stress.

Responses to stress
When we are under physical or psychological pressure, our bodies respond with the "fight or flight" reflex to enable us to deal with the confrontation. During this reflex, adrenalin is released into the body and the heart begins to pound, the rate of breathing increases, blood pressure rises, the pupils enlarge and the blood sugar level rises so that a large amount of energy will be available if needed.

Because we rarely need to fight or flee, the body remains tensed for action that never takes place. If this response constantly occurs, it can cause a number of physical and psychological illnesses and can aggravate pre-existing conditions. Constant stress is also a contributory factor in the development of serious disorders such as high blood pressure, heart disease, asthma and diabetes, and an association between stress and cancer has been suggested.

Symptoms of stress
The classic signs of stress are recognizable enough. These include headaches, ulcer flare-ups, temper outbursts, impatience, stomach pains and upsets, sleep disorders, menstrual disorders, and digestive upsets. You may notice that you are eating, smoking or drinking more than usual, or that you have lost your appetite and are unable to eat.

STRESS RELIEF

Everybody needs help coping with the effects of physical, mental or emotional stress at some time or another. There are a number of different methods to help ease and alleviate stress, and gentle exercise is one of the best. This program will help your muscles to relax and your mind to slow down. Gradually you will begin to breathe quietly and deeply.

Stand with your feet 15cm (6in) apart. Stretch up and forwards until your hands are resting on a high shelf or window sash. Breathe out and feel your spine stretch from your tailbone towards your head. Continue to breathe slowly and after each out-breath feel the tension ease in your shoulders and upper back. Hold for up to 1 minute.

Now stand up straight. Link your fingers together, palms out, and as you breathe in extend your arms to shoulder level. As you breathe out take them up above your head. Breathe deeply, maintaining the stretch in your spine (left). Keep your feet firmly planted on the floor, toes spread out, and feel yourself stretch very tall. Hold for a few seconds. Breathing out let your arms drop and relax your shoulders (right). Stand straight and breathe deeply for a minute or two without straining.

First kneel on all fours. On an out-breath straighten your legs and take your hips up and back, keeping your back straight.

Then take your heels down to the floor. Hold this position for about 30 seconds, then come back on to all fours.

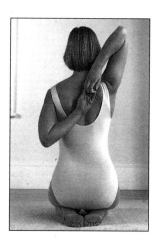

Sit on your heels on a rug, with your knees together. Dropping your shoulders, stretch one arm up and bring the other up behind your back (left). Catch your hands as shown but do not drop your head forwards. Hold for a few seconds, then change hands. Afterwards, sit quietly on your heels for a minute or two with shoulders relaxed and eyes closed, and clasping your hands behind you (right). This will relax tight muscles in your neck.

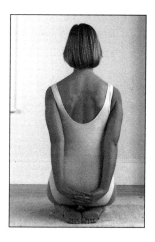

Finally lie flat on your back, stretching out your legs from your hips to your heels. As you breathe out, let the weight of your body sink into the floor. Release tension in your shoulders by letting them drop down to the floor. Breathe gently and evenly. Stay in this position for at least 10 to 15 minutes.

Your body also tells you in more subtle ways that it is under duress. Certain skin conditions will flare up, get worse or temporarily stop responding to treatment. If you are prone to acne, you may find that breakouts occur during stressful times. Eczema and psoriasis, which are skin disorders characterized by redness and scaling, and itching in the case of eczema, can flare up during time of duress. Hair can also start to fall out, usually in patches or clumps. The lips, gums and teeth also respond to stress; cold sores or fever blisters may appear, or the gums may beome tender and bleed.

Coping with stress

Stress control is an important factor for good health. How and where you live and work can make a noticeable difference to the amount of stress in your life. The continual noise, traffic congestion and pollution of today's urban environments are one of the major sources of stress. Eliminating these sources as much as possible will help to reduce the amount of unnecessary stress in your life. Each of us finds our own way of coping with stress in our lives, but following are some suggestions that may help everyone.

- Make sure you get enough rest. About eight hours a night is the right amount for most people to be at their best.
- Get regular exercise, choosing one that you enjoy. Exercise almost always counteracts stress and tension and leaves you feeling more relaxed and rational about your problems.
- Eat a balanced and nutritious diet. Limit the amount of caffeine you have, as too much can make you tense and jittery.
- Put a stressful situation into perspective. Ask yourself if you are overreacting to small stressful situations, such as traffic jams, missed appointments, or minor family arguments.
- Look at the way you manage your time. Your stress may be caused by disorganization and the fact that you are getting behind in your work or household chores. You may have to reorganize your priorities and do the important tasks first.
- Recognize your limitations and take on only what you can accomplish in the amount of time you have allowed yourself. Setting up and meeting realistic goals can lessen stress, while failing to live up to your expectations can bring it about.
- Talk about your problems with your family or friends. This will help to lighten the load and reduce stress that is associated with coping alone.
- Be sure and make time for yourself and have some fun, either by spending time by yourself or with friends in relaxing environment. Happy people cope with stress better than bored, unhappy people.
- If you find that you are not coping very well and are unable to deal with the pressures yourself, seek professional help. Your doctor may be able to offer some advice, or refer you to a therapist or counsellor who can offer a sympathetic ear and some professional advice.

FACE CARE

Beautiful skin is more often due to your genes than a result of the types of creams and lotions you put on it. This doesn't mean that your skin, no matter what type, cannot be improved by eating a proper diet, getting regular exercise, and developing and maintaining a skin care routine. And it is never too young to start caring for your skin, since the benefits will last a lifetime.

THE STRUCTURE OF SKIN

The skin is made up of four layers; the horny outer layer, which consists of dead cells; the epidermis; the dermis; and the subcutaneous layer of fat. The skin is designed to be waterproof, and nothing that is put on the skin, such as moisturizers, cellular renewal creams or anti-ageing creams, can penetrate any deeper than the outermost layers of the epidermis.

Skin grows from within outwards. This occurs at the basal cell layer, which separates the dermis from the epidermis. These cells are continuously reproducing and moving forward towards the skin's surface. When these cells die, they form the horny layer that acts as a safety barrier and protects the

SKIN STRUCTURE

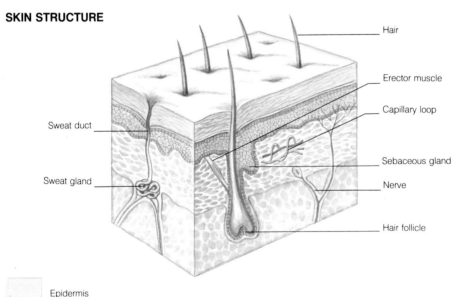

Epidermis

Dermis

Subcutaneous layer

The skin consists of four layers. The outer layer is made up of dead cells, the epidermis contains sweat glands and hair follicles, the dermis contains the blood vessels, and the subcutaneous layer contains protective fat. Nothing that is put in the skin can penetrate deeper than the epidermis.

fresh cells underneath. At the surface these cells form keratin, a layer of tough material that is thickest in body areas subject to the most wear and tear, such as the palms of the hands and the soles of the feet. The surface layer is in a constant state of renewal as the dead cells are sloughed off and replaced by other cells. Exfoliation removes this surface layer, leaving the skin smooth.

Collagen, the elastic tissue in the dermis layer, gives the skin its suppleness, smoothness, and plumpness. As you age, the collagen tissues break down, which causes skin to sag, wrinkle, and thin. Nothing short of cosmetic surgery can prevent these signs of ageing. The rate at which your skin ages is inherited, so if your parents have young-looking skin, chances are you will too.

DETERMINING YOUR SKIN TYPE

Each person's skin is individual but tends to fall into one of four main types; dry, oily, combination, or sensitive, depending on the level of activity of the sebaceous glands. Your skin type will determine the texture of your skin and what kind of skin care routine you need.

Women who are fair complexioned and light haired usually have dry skin. Such skin has little natural oil due to underactive sebaceous glands, it burns easily in the sun, and is frequently also sensitive. Dry skin is usually very fine and has few visible pores; it often develops flaky patches in cold weather. It is frequently affected by temperature changes, artificial heating or air conditioning, and air pollution. Women with dry skin rarely have acne as a teenager, but as they get older the lack of natural lubrication can cause fine lines and wrinkles to develop prematurely. The most important aspect of caring for dry skin is to moisturize it regularly.

Dark haired, dark skinned women often have oily skin, which is the result of overactive sebaceous glands. Oily skin is prone to breakouts, and often has a shiny film all over, particularly on the nose and cheeks. It is frequently large pored and coarser looking than dry skin. Although younger girls with oily skin often find they have continual breakouts and acne, oily skin is less likely to wrinkle early.

Most women have combination skin, which has areas of both dryness and oiliness. The greasy patches are usually down the centre of the face, forming a T shape, while the remainder of the skin on the face is drier, finer in texture, and in need of more moisturizing. If the difference between the two areas is great they should be treated with separate skin care products.

Women who have sensitive skin find that it is usually dry, delicate, and prone to broken capillaries and allergic reactions such as rashes. With sensitive skin, it is important to use products designed for this specific skin type; these products are laboratory tested to eliminate ingredients that are known to cause allergies and are often termed hypoallergenic.

DEVELOPING A SKIN CARE ROUTINE

There are many products on the market these days that promise to give you younger looking skin, to remove wrinkles, and to perform miracles. No skin care product can do this. As it cannot penetrate below the surface of the skin, it cannot remove wrinkles that are already established, and it cannot push back the clock and eliminate any signs of ageing. But this isn't to say that you cannot improve your skin and make it look as good as you possibly can. With this in mind, it is important to develop and maintain a good skin care routine from an early age.

The most important thing to remember is to use products that are designed for your skin type. Some products, such as astringent toners designed for oily skin, will be much too harsh if used on dry skin, and moisturizers for dry skin will be too heavy and greasy for oily skin. Once you have chosen your products, it is easy to organize a simple cleansing, toning and moisturizing routine that takes only minutes to perform both morning and night.

Cleansing

This is the first step in your routine. Morning and evening are usually the best times for cleansing, although if you are going out in the evening and reapplying makeup, always clean your face first. There is such a wide range of facial cleansers on the market today, formulated for various types of skin, that you will soon discover the one that suits you best. The decision as to which type of cleanser you choose is a personal one, but it is important that you select a product that is right for your skin.

Women used to believe that soap and water should be used to clean the face, but soap is drying and defatting, and should not be used on the face unless your skin is very oily. Special soapless cleansing bars are perfect if you love the feel of soap and water. These are designed to be gentle on the skin, particularly dry skin. Other cleansers that foam up when combined with water are available – these are ideal if you dislike the feeling of cream. But don't forget that hard water alone is defatting and dries out the skin.

There is a wide variety of cleansing creams and lotions available. These are probably the best way to clean, as they are gentle on the skin and contain none of the harsh ingredients that some of the other forms of cleansers have. Most cleansing lotions are intended to be applied to the skin and then wiped off with clean cotton wool pads or tissues; others are rinsed off with water and a flannel.

Cleansers, toners and moisturizers in the form of creams, bars, lotions and liquids are formulated for different skin types (overleaf).

After cleansing, make sure that any residue of cleanser is thoroughly removed. With facial bars or soaps, rinse your face repeatedly to remove any film that might have adhered to the skin. If your face still feels sticky, wipe over it again with dampened cotton wool pads – if it doesn't come away clean, rinse again. If using a cream or lotion, wipe the face with a dampened cotton wool pad to make sure that all the cream is removed.

10 MINUTE SKIN CARE

Once you have developed your daily skin care routine it should only take a few minutes every morning and night. Be sure that the products you use are correct for your skin type.

▶ Always remove eye makeup before going to bed. Dampen a cotton wool pad or ball with remover and wipe over the eye area. Do this gently and never pull or tug at the skin around the eyes, which is very delicate. You may need to go over the lids and lashes a few times until all traces of makeup are gone.

▲ Next cleanse your face thoroughly. If you suffer from spots or acne you may find using a complexion brush helps to unblock pores.

▲ Tone your skin with the appropriate formulation, then apply a light film of moisturizer. Gently massage it in and tissue off any excess.

▲ Moisturize your neck and throat, too, as the skin in these areas can easily become dry. Work the moisturizer up from the throat towards the jaw.

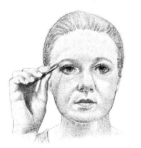

◀ Always pluck your brows from underneath the natural arch and in the direction of the hair's growth.

▶ Apply one of the special eye creams that reduce morning puffiness and swelling. These are usually made from herb extracts.

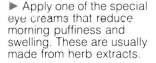

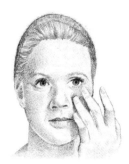

FACE CARE

Toning

Toners, often called skin tonics and fresheners, are the second step in a skin care routine. Their job is to remove any remaining grease, dirt or makeup left after cleansing. Proper toning will also refresh your skin, making it feel cool and clean.

All toners are liquid, but there are various formulations, depending on the amount of alcohol they contain, available for all types of skin. Some are particularly good for dry skin, being alcohol free, while others have astringent properties that are particularly good for greasy skin and help to remove excess oil. To use a toner, just apply it to a cotton wool ball or pad and wipe over the face, avoiding the eye area and lips.

Moisturizing

Every day skin loses some of its natural moisture. This process, called dehydration, is made worse by extreme temperatures, central heating and air conditioning. A moisturizer is probably the most important skin care product you can use, as it helps to slow down the normal dehydration process by creating a fine film on the skin's surface to prevent moisture from escaping. Moisturizers are what help to keep the skin smooth, soft and elastic, and gives it a fresh youthful look.

The majority of moisturizers are emulsions of oil and water. The oil-in-water moisturizers have a higher water content and are lighter and less heavy; these are good for use during the day when makeup will be applied over it, or for women with oily skin. The water-in-oil types consist of more oil than water, and are usually used at night when it is important to slow down the dehydration process or for women with very dry skin. As with all skin care products, choose a moisturizer for your skin type. Ask the salesperson at the cosmetics counter to recommend the appropriate moisturizer.

A moisturizer should be applied after cleansing and toning. Don't apply it heavily, as only a light film is needed, and don't apply moisturizer around the eye area as it can cause the delicate skin in this area to retain fluid and become puffy. Don't forget to use it on your neck and throat, which can become dry and dehydrated just like the skin on your face. Always wait a few minutes after applying moisturizer before putting on your makeup; this allows time for it to dry and form a smooth base for your foundation.

Eye makeup removers

The normal cleansing and toning routine is only to be used on the facial skin, and should not be used around the eye area, where the skin is very thin and delicate. To remove eye makeup, there are gels, lotions and creams that are specially designed for this purpose. If you wear contact lenses seek out special eye makeup removers that will not smear on the lenses. If you use water resistant or waterproof eye makeup, the product you use must be oil based to be effective, and should be used sparingly.

To remove eye makeup, go over the lids and lashes with cotton wool pads dampened with remover, and keep cleaning until there is no makeup left on the pads. Never pull at the delicate tissues around the eyes – treat the skin in this area gently. When all eye makeup is removed, dampen a cotton wool ball and gently wipe over the eye area. This will remove any residual oil and prevent the eyes from being puffy in the morning.

After all your eye makeup is removed, apply eye gel or cream in sparing amounts around the eye. These are specifically made to be used in the area around the eyes to add extra moisture and protect the tissues. A number of these products can also be used during the day and can be worn under makeup to provide a smooth base.

PERSONAL SKIN CARE PLAN

	Oily skin	Combination skin	Dry skin
Objective	To counteract overactive sebaceous glands without dehydrating the skin.	To reduce oil in greasy areas without stripping oil from dry areas.	To replenish the oil and to prevent moisture from evaporating.
Cleanser	Choose an oil-free soap or a water-soluble lotion. Cleanse at least twice a day.	Choose a creamy lotion with a light oil agent or a soapless cleansing bar. Cleanse twice a day.	Choose a creamy lotion or a soapless cleansing bar. Cleanse once or twice a day.
Toner	Choose a toner containing alcohol; use it twice a day.	Choose a gentle low-alcohol toner; use it twice a day.	Choose an extra mild alcohol-free toner; use it once a day.
Moisturizer	Use a light, water-based moisturizer once a day; twice a day in winter.	Use a light, hydrating formula twice a day.	Use a rich hydrating formula containing oil two or three times a day.
Exfoliant	Use an oil-absorbing scrub every other day; do not exfoliate acne.	Use a gentle scrub mask two or three times a week.	Use a cream-based mild scrub once a week.

SPECIAL TREATMENTS

Your daily skin care routine is designed to keep your skin healthy and clean, but there are a number of special treatments that can be used on an occasional basis to keep your skin in ideal condition.

The treatments you need and the frequency with which you perform them depends on your skin type, your age, and whether or not you have any skin problems. Never use scrubs or masks if you have spots as you will spread the infection.

Face masks

Face masks come in packs, gels, creams and lotions. These are applied to the skin, left to dry, and then peeled or washed off. They perform a variety of functions, and can be used to moisturize, deep clean, or act as an exfoliant. Most masks can be used once a week.

Types of mask

Moisturizing masks often have an herbal content and are cream based. They are very gentle and are ideal for dry or sensitive skin. Cleansing masks are clay-based, and are best for oily skin as they dry out the skin and help to draw out excess oil. They dry to form a firm hard mask and should be removed with lukewarm water. Exfoliating masks are often gels or creams. When they dry, they are gently peeled or rubbed off with the fingertips, and remove the top layer of dead skin cells as the same time.

Applying masks

Masks should always be applied to clean, dry skin. Tie your hair back off the face, then apply the mask with the fingertips, avoiding the eyes and lips. Spread the mask evenly over the skin, working it upwards and outwards. You may want to lie down with dampened cotton wool pads over the eyes and rest while the mask is working. Leave it on the skin for the recommended time, then remove according to the manufacturer's instructions. Whichever mask you choose, always apply it according to the instructions, and do not leave the mask on for longer than the suggested time. Always wait a couple of hours after using a mask before applying makeup to allow the skin to settle.

Exfoliation

Regular cleansing helps to remove some of the dead skin cells from the face, but some always remain which can give the face a dull, lifeless appearance. Exfoliation is the process of sloughing off the dead skin cells, which are then replaced by fresh cells underneath. If this is done regularly, it will speed up the turnover and replacement of cells, which helps to open blocked pores. Exfoliation makes the skin feel smoother and softer, it improves the texture, and makes the skin look fresh and clean.

Special skin treatments include face masks, cleansing grains, and various exfoliants (right).

25 MINUTE FACIAL

A facial is one of the best ways to keep your skin in good condition and can easily be done at home. It takes less than half an hour from start to finish and can include a massage.

◀ First thoroughly cleanse and tone your skin. You can then steam your face to open your pores. This makes it easier to remove any blackheads.

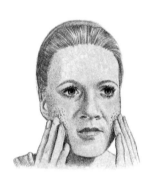

▶ Exfoliation helps to remove the top layer of dead skin. Gently rub the exfoliator over your skin in circular motions, avoiding the lips and eye area.

▶ Apply a mask all over your face, avoiding the lips and eye area. Some masks harden when dry and are washed off, while others dry to a thin gel that is peeled off. Lie down with your feet up and relax while the mask is working. Leave it on only for the recommended amount of time.

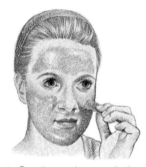

▲ Gently peel or wash the mask off the skin. Dampen a cotton wool ball with toner and wipe it over your face to remove any residue of mask and apply moisturizer.

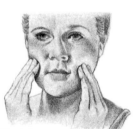

▲ Facial massage can improve the tone and circulation of the skin. Apply cream and work in small circular movements.

▲ Continue by kneading the skin of the cheeks, mouth and chin area.

Using a complexion brush when cleansing your face is one method of exfoliation, as is the exfoliating facial mask. Best of all are the special cleansing grains and facial scrubs that are designed to gently slough off dead skin. Most of these contain tiny particles of natural ingredients and feel slightly rough to the touch. The grains and particles create gentle friction that scrubs away the dead skin cells, and can be used on all types of skin, although they should be used less frequently on dry or sensitive skin.

Using exfoliants

Exfoliants leave the skin feeling very smooth, but they may stimulate the sebaceous glands and leave the skin oilier than before. Most are intended to be used once a week – they should not be used daily. Exfoliation should always be done after cleansing the face. Most exfoliants are applied to slightly dampened skin; follow the manufacturer's instructions for this. Apply a thin layer of exfoliant on the skin, avoiding the eye and lip area. Rub gently, using circular motions, then tissue away or rinse off the excess. Always apply moisturizer after exfoliation.

Home facials

Most beauty salons offer a professional facial, but you can easily give yourself one at home. First cleanse your face thoroughly, then tone it. Steam open your pores to make blackhead removal easier by placing your face over a bowl of hot water and covering your head with a towel. Keep your face about 48cm away from the steaming water. After about five minutes of steaming your skin will be soft and your pores open. You should then be able to remove any blackheads using clean fingertips or a special blackhead remover. As the final step, apply a gentle face mask such as a moisturizing mask, place some dampened cotton wool pads over your eyes and lie down for about 10-15 minutes. Remove the mask as directed and apply moisturizer.

COPING WITH SKIN PROBLEMS

Almost all women have suffered from annoying little bumps, blemishes, or blackheads and whiteheads at some time in their lives. Many of these can be treated at home with certain cleansing and care routines, but others may require the help and advice of a doctor or dermatologist (see chart on page 36). The most common skin complaints are blackheads, whiteheads, pimples, broken veins and allergic reactions.

Allergic reactions, such as hives, rashes or patchy dryness, occur frequently on the face. This may be due to a food that has been eaten, or some sort of cosmetic preparation that is being put on the skin. Discuss the problem with your doctor, who may refer you to an allergy specialist or a dermatologist to determine the cause.

COMMON SKIN PROBLEMS

Problem	Cause	Treatment
Acne	Acne is caused by the blockage of the exit from the sebaceous gland, which will eventually rupture and release sebum (oil) into the deeper layers of the skin. This oil is an irritant, which causes inflammation of the gland that then becomes infected. Acne is not caused by diet.	You should cleanse your face thoroughly if you have acne, and an antibacterial cleanser may help. Exposure to sunlight may also help, as this makes the skin peel and unblocks the sebaceous glands. If severe, consult your doctor who may prescribe antibiotics or special cleansers.
Blackheads	Blackheads are caused by sebum (oil) accumulation in the pores. Oil rises to the surface of the skin, where it oxidizes and darkens.	You can remove blackheads at home. Steam your face for a few minutes to open the pores, then squeeze the blackhead gently between the fingertips or use a blackhead remover. Regular use of an exfoliator helps to prevent clogged pores.
Broken veins	The tendency to broken veins is inherited and they cannot be prevented. Broken veins are actually tiny capillaries that are close to the surface of the skin, usually around the cheeks and nose.	Broken veins can often be treated by electrodessication, a procedure that uses high-frequency electrical current to destroy tissue. This must be done by a professional, and broken veins may return.
Moles	Moles are due to heredity, and some don't appear until after the age of 20. During the development of the skin, melanocytes (pigment-producing cells) collect together in small patches. With age, moles get larger and increase in number.	Moles can sometimes be removed by cosmetic surgery. A local anaesthetic is used to numb the area and the dermatologist then scrapes off the mole at the skin's surface. The scab that forms heals within a week, leaving no scar.
Skin tags	These small appendages of skin, which are usually found on the neck, shoulders and underarms, are due to heredity. They usually increase with age.	Skin tags can be removed by using electrodessication (see broken veins). Tiny scabs form and the area usually heals within a week.
Spots	Spots may be part of acne, and they may also appear in some women before their period due to higher hormone levels.	Unless pus is present, never squeeze or try and remove a spot. Once pus has formed expel it using clean fingertips.
Whiteheads	Whiteheads (milia) are small sweat spots and are not part of acne. They are cysts of the sebaceous or sweat glands in areas where oil secretion is low. The gland does not burst as in acne, but the oil becomes thick, hard and white.	Whiteheads can be removed at home. Use a sterile needle to prick the skin over the whitehead, then very gently squeeze out the secretion. Cleanse the skin afterwards with antiseptic cream.
Wrinkles	Wrinkles are caused by the breakdown of collagen, either with age or through chronic exposure to the sun.	Wrinkles cannot be prevented or treated. Cosmetic surgery, such as a face lift, can tighten the skin. The effect lasts from two to five years, depending on the woman.

HAIR CARE

Healthy shining hair makes you feel wonderful and is a great confidence booster. Just washing your hair can lift your spirits, and a new hairstyle that suits you perfectly can make all the difference to the way you see yourself and to the way others see you.

When it comes to your hair, you don't have to settle for what nature has given you. Your hair is one of your most versatile features, and it is possible to change its style, condition, colour, and even texture to give yourself a completely new and different look.

THE STRUCTURE OF HAIR

Hair grows from a follicle that is located below the surface of the skin. The hair shaft, which is the only part we see, is composed mainly of keratin and is entirely dead.

Each hair has a spongy inner core, the medulla, which is surrounded by a stronger layer called the cortex. The cortex is responsible for the strength, thickness, and flexibility of the hair. It also contains melanin, the pigment that determines hair colour. Any product designed to bring about permanent change, such as bleaches, tints and perms, must penetrate the cortex to restructure a hair's characteristics. The cortex is protected by the cuticle, which is a transparent layer of tiny, overlapping scales of keratin. When the hair is in good condition the keratin scales will be shiny and lie flat; if your hair is tangled, dry or damaged the scales will be ruffled, which will give your hair a dull appearance and a rough texture.

Hair growth

The hair root is the fastest growing organ in the body; hair on the scalp grows at the rate of about one half inch a month. Hair does not grow at a constant rate. It grows faster in summer than in winter, and grows at different rates over the head. The growth rate for each person varies. The cycle, which is the time between the first growth of hair and its final shedding, generally lasts for between three to five years, but may go on much longer. When the cycle is over, the follicle shrinks and goes into a resting phase that lasts for a few months. The old hair stops getting longer and simply remains in the follicle until a new hair forms underneath and pushes it out.

The average person sheds about 100 hairs each day. Fortunately, the growth and resting cycles are not synchronized in adjacent follicles and you do not notice any obvious patches of hair loss. Some people find it difficult to grow their hair long, while others find it very easy. This is the result of your particular combination of growth rate and hair life span – only if your hair has a fast growth rate and a long life span can you quickly and successfully grow your hair long.

There are between 100,000 and 150,000 hairs growing on the head at any one time. Redheads have the least amount of strands but the thickest hair, while blondes have the most amount but the finest hair. This total number decreases as you get older, as some follicles wear out and are not replaced. The rate at which you lose hair is genetically determined and cannot be halted.

The photograph (right) shows a view of the cut ends of normal hair, in which the different layers of the hair shaft are clearly visible. The thin outer protective layer, the cuticle, is made up of scales of a fibrous protein called keratin. When hair is in good condition the keratin scales lie smoothly on top of each other so that they overlap. When hair is mistreated or neglected the scales becomes curled at the edges and distorted. The inner thicker layer, the cortex, surrounds the central core of the hair, the medulla. The pigments that determine hair colour are found in the cortex, and if a permanent colour change is desired the chemicals used must be able to penetrate this layer.

A healthy hair immediately after it has been washed in shampoo is clean and free of any grease and dirt.

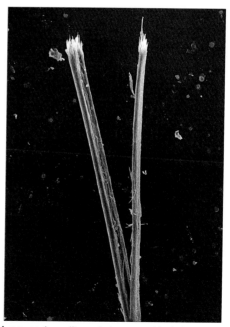

A severely split and damaged hair is an indication of serious maltreatment. The shaft is split in two and the ends look like a frayed paintbrush.

DETERMINING YOUR HAIR TYPE

The type of hair you have dictates the kind of care and style it needs. The texture of hair is genetically determined. Each individual hair may be coarse, fine, thick or curly. Your hair's type and texture will affect its care and condition and also determine the styles that will suit you best.

Hair texture

Hair may be coarse, fine, frizzy or thick. You may have a lot of hair follicles on your head, giving you a thick head of hair, or you may have fewer, giving you fine, flyaway hair. The thickness of the individual hairs also varies from person to person; these factors will determine your hair care routine.

The amount of natural curl in a hair depends on the shape of the hair follicles. Straight hair grows from a follicle that is more or less round, and the hair itself is round in cross section. Wavy hair is kidney-shaped in cross section, and the amount of wave in the hair depends on the degree of curve in the follicle. Curly hair grows from a very curved hair follicle.

Hair condition

Although no two people have the same hair, most people's hair falls into one of three categories; dry, normal, or oily. These categories are determined by the amount of oil produced by the sebaceous glands, which are located at the top of each hair follicle close to the scalp surface. This oil is necessary to healthy hair, as it coats the hair in a fine layer, providing sheen and elasticity.

Dry hair

Dry hair occurs when the sebaceous glands produce too little oil to keep the surface of the hair supple and shiny. Dry hair looks dull and brittle, and often feels rough to the touch; it often splits easily and loses elasticity.

Dry hair may be caused artificially, from overprocessing and overheating, from too much sunlight, too much perming and bleaching, or overfrequent washing. Dry hair has little natural protection and regular conditioning is essential. A weekly deep moisturizing treatment is recommended to keep dry hair in good condition, and ends need regular trimming to avoid splitting

Oily hair

Oily hair generally goes hand in hand with oily skin. It is due to overproduction from the sebaceous glands, which coats the hair with excess oil and makes it lank and lifeless within a day or so of washing. The grease attracts dust, so oily hair needs frequent washing. Use a mild shampoo if you wash your hair daily, as the hair requires a certain amount of natural oil if it is to stay healthy and elastic. Hair may become more oily during times of illness or stress. Only comb or brush it when necessary, and do not play with the hair or rub the scalp, since this only stimulates the sebaceous glands.

Normal hair

Normal hair is as much the result of good luck as it is careful treatment. It has a natural gloss and shine and feels soft and smooth to the touch. Always use mild shampoos and conditioners, and at the first sign of any problems, take the necessary steps to protect your hair.

Combination hair

This type of hair is oily at the scalp and dry at the ends. It occurs more in oily long hair that has damaged ends. It can also occur to people with dandruff as the oil soaks into the dry flakes on the scalp instead of travelling along the hair shaft. Use a mild shampoo and condition the ends of the hair only, leaving the scalp free from this type of treatment.

DEVELOPING A HAIR CARE ROUTINE

Your hair care routine should be planned for your specific hair type. The basics include shampooing, conditioning, and special treatments.

Shampooing

Regular hair washing is essential today, due partly to the increase in dust, grime and dirt, and also because of the various products we use to dress our hair. Together, these contribute to produce a surface film on the hair that must be removed if the hair is to stay clean, fresh and shiny.

The scalp should be treated as gently as possible and a mild shampoo should always be used. You may need to experiment with various shampoos until you find the one that suits you best. And it is a good idea to change your shampoo occasionally; your hair and scalp get used to its action, and after a time it may not work as well as it once did.

There are a number of shampoos on the market, designed for every type of hair. Look for one that is formulated for your hair type. A shampoo should cleanse throughly without irritating or demoisturizing the scalp.

To shampoo properly:

- Brush or comb the hair thoroughly to loosen dirt and dead skin cells from the scalp.
- Wet the hair completely, making sure that the underneath layers are well saturated.
- Pour a small amount of shampoo, about a teaspoonful, into your palm. Wet the shampoo first to dilute it, as most are concentrated formulas.
- Massage the shampoo gently into the hair roots with the fingertips, covering the whole scalp. Start at the scalp and work through to the ends.
- With the flat of your hand, work the shampoo into the bulk of the hair over the top layers. This shouldn't take too long, as shampoo need only be in contact with the hair for half a minute to clean thoroughly.

Shampoos, conditioners, mousses and gels are made for dry, oily, permed and coloured hair (overleaf).

30 MINUTE HAIR CARE

Clean hair makes you feel terrific. Keep your hair healthy and shiny with regular shampooing and conditioning. Be sure to treat hair very gently when it is wet.

◄ Place a small amount of shampoo in the palm of your hand. Wet it slightly to dilute it, then massage gently into the scalp using your fingertips.

► Use lukewarm water to rinse out all the shampoo, as any left on your hair may leave it looking dull and lifeless. Then blot your hair with a towel.

► While your hair is still damp, gently comb through or massage in conditioner and leave it on for the specified amount of time. Rinse it out thoroughly, or your hair may become sticky and greasy.

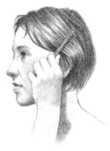

▲ For dry hair, apply a deep conditioning treatment before shampooing. Then wrap a warm towel around the head for 15-30 minutes, changing the towel as necessary.

▲ Always keep a blow dryer at least 6 inches away from your hair. To scrunch dry, bunch up some hair in your hand and direct the heat on to the hair between your fingers.

► To style your hair using a blow dryer you may want to use a brush. Wrap a small section of hair around the brush. Direct the heat on to the brush and hold it steady until the hair is dry. Start with a warm setting and switch to a cooler one as each section dries.

- Rinse your hair thoroughly with lukewarm water and check that there is no shampoo left in your hair.
- Blot the hair with a towel. Never rub it, as hair is at its weakest when wet and has less elasticity.
- Wrap your hair in a towel and leave the towel to absorb the moisture. When the hair is damp rather than wet, comb it through with a wide-toothed comb and dry it in the usual way.

Conditioning

The main purpose of any conditioner is to restore the electrical balance of the hair. Conditioners also smooth the scales of the cuticle, making the hair less liable to tangle, and give hair a better sheen when dry. Conditioners can bring bounce, body, shine and manageability back to hair that would otherwise be dull. They can also help to seal each hair, guarding against water evaporation, which is the major cause of dryness.

There are conditioners in different strengths for every type of hair. The instant conditioners are massaged in and then immediately rinsed off while others are left on the hair for a longer period of time and work in conjunction with heat to provide extra help. Conditioners only provide temporary relief from dryness as the hair cannot be permanently mended once it has grown out of the scalp, but they are a vital part of the hair care routine and should be used regularly.

Instant conditioners

The instant conditioners, or cream rinses as they were once called, are intended to be used after every shampoo. They coat each hair with a fine film that corrects dryness and superficially mends any damage. Once the hair has been washed the conditioner is massaged in, left on for a few minutes, then rinsed off thoroughly.

Only a small amount of conditioner is needed. If you use too much conditioner or fail to rinse the hair well you may find your hair has become sticky and greasy. Don't overcondition your hair or it may become too soft and impossible to curl. If your hair is particularly dry at the ends, apply conditioner to those areas only and leave the naturally healthy hair at the roots alone.

Deep conditioning treatments

In addition to instant conditioners, there are deep penetrating conditioners that are meant for occasional use. These deep conditioners are especially useful for dry or processed hair or hair that has been damaged by too much time spent in the sun.

Creamy deep conditioning treatments are massaged into the hair and left on the hair from anywhere from 10 to 30 minutes; follow the manufacturer's instructions. When you are massaging the conditioner in, pay particular

attention to the drier areas. To gain the maximum benefit from this treatment, leave the cream on the hair after massaging, wrap the head in foil to retain heat and let the treatment continue. Rinse your hair thoroughly with warm water to remove all of the conditioner.

Hot oil treatments are just as efficient, and are especially good for dry hair. You can buy small tubes of oil treatment or just use almond oil. Warm the oil, then apply it to the hair. Massage it in well and wrap the head in plastic wrap or foil. Cover the head with a warm towel and leave for half an hour; the heat from the towel helps the oil to penetrate. Then shampoo the hair and rinse thoroughly. For an even better treatment, leave the oil on overnight. Then wash it out with two applications of shampoo and condition as usual. If your hair is dry or damaged, use a hot oil treatment once a week. For normal or oily hair once or twice a month should be sufficient.

BLOW DRYING METHODS

Unless you have a wash and wear style, blow drying will play an important part in how your finished style looks. A blow dryer can create a wide variety of looks, and help to straighten hair that is too curly or frizzy. The new hair dryers have a number of attachments. Some come with various blower speeds and three temperature settings. Some have circular brush attachments, which avoid the need for a separate brush.

Always hold a blow dryer at least six inches away from the hair – this way the heat will be less damaging. And keep the hair dryer moving to avoid overheating the hair in one area. Use a full or half radial styling brush to shape your hair as you dry it, or choose one of the dryers that comes with its own brush attachment.

If your hair is wavy or if you have a perm, it is best to let the hair dry naturally. For a short ragged cut, finger dry the hair by pushing the hair into place and dry with a hand-held dryer. With very curly or layered styles, scrunch drying is used. Hold a handful of hair tightly bunched up in the hand and direct the heat from the dryer on to the hair between the fingers.

If you have a style that needs thorough blow drying to look its best, always roughly towel dry the hair first until it is slightly damp. Divide the hair into small sections, keeping the hair you are not working on out of the way by clipping it back with pins. Roll each section around the brush and hold it steady until the hair is dry. Start with a hot setting and switch to cold as each section dries.

The underneath sections should be dried first, then the sides. Lift the brush to give your hair more bounce and to speed up the drying process. Brush from underneath to curl the hair in, from above for flicked up curls. Unpin the other sections and gradually blend in the layers as you dry. Dry the front and your fringe last.

ombs, brushes,
rlers, rollers, dryers
d tongs will help
u get the hairstyle
u want (left)

USING ROLLERS

Rollers can give your hair body and volume, and are essential for a neat set on hair that has been permed. They are used with a setting lotion or mousse to help hold the set. The size of the roller will determine the size of the curl or wave. Do not roll too much hair around individual rollers, as the finished effect will be uneven.

If using sponge or plastic rollers, dry your hair with a dryer or leave it to dry naturally. Make sure that the hair is completely dry before removing the rollers or the result will be frizzy and hard to manage. After removing the rollers and clips, brush through firmly to smooth out any curl lines.

Heated rollers are always used on dry hair and can be used with setting lotion. Although the temperature is controlled, overuse can damage or dry the hair, so do not use them every day. Heat them for the specified time, then roll up the hair and leave them until the roller is cool. If you take them out halfway through the curl will not last for very long.

USING CURLING TONGS AND BRUSHES

These take much longer to use, since only one section of hair can be curled at a time. They are ideal for curling small sections of hair, such as flicked back sides or fringes. Although the effect is not as long lasting as an ordinary roller set, they are quick and convenient to use. The rods and brushes can get overheated very quickly so care must be taken.

Wind sections of hair around the rod or brush and hold it steady for the recommended time. Some curling tongs have a spiked surface that can get tangled in the hair, as can the hot brushes. Make sure that your hair is sectioned really well and the hair kept away from each end of the spikes. Tongs give a tighter curl than rollers, while hot brushes give a loose, bouncy style but, again, overuse can be extremely drying to the hair.

MOUSSES, GELS AND SPRAYS

Many hair styles today depend on height and shape, and a number of products are now on the market to help you achieve this.

Mousse

Mousse is applied to towel-dried hair after shampooing, and worked through the hair so that it coats every strand. The hair is then set or blow dried in the usual way. Only a small amount of mousse is needed, about the size of an egg, as more can be added later. Mousse is particularly good for curly hair, as it gives the hair a lift from the root and doesn't straighten the natural curl.

Hair accessories such as combs, clips, ribbons and bows can be used to dress up or change your look (right).

Some mousses now contain colorant so that you can try out special effects for parties. They will wash out within a couple of shampoos, unless your hair is extremely dry and porous through the long term use of bleaches.

Gel

Styling gels are completely different than mousses. Most gels are used on towel-dried hair, and then the hair is combed into shape or arranged with the fingers. Gels dry quite stiff, and firmly hold the hair in place once it has dried. They make the hair look very glossy and shiny, giving hair a "wet look", and are best used on straight hair that is cut short or layered. Gels can flake out of the hair on to the scalp, and should be brushed out each night. Your hair may need to be washed more often if you use gel regularly.

Setting lotions and sprays

Setting lotions help hold the shape of the hair once it is dry. These are applied on clean, towel-dried hair. Setting agents give the hair more body and bounce, and are especially effective on fine hair. Most lotions come in different weight "holds". The lighter versions are best suited to casual relaxed hairstyles, while the firmer ones are used on hair that needs real control.

Hair spray can be used to hold the shape and set of the hair and also comes in various holds. There is a tendency to overuse hair spray, and hair can become hard looking and lacking in movement and swing. Hair spray is most often used on hair that has been set, dried, and brushed into style. Spray the hair lightly, then arrange the finishing touches with your fingertips. This makes for a more natural result than just spraying the hair and leaving the spray to set. Brush hairspray out of the hair every night, otherwise it can cause dryness and damage.

Using hair accessories

Hair ornaments and decorations, such as clips, combs and ribbons, help to add the finishing touch to your hairstyle. Some are simple and plain, while others are dazzling and ornate. When wearing hair accessories, choose ones that blend in with the colours of your clothes but make certain they will stand out against your hair colour. Dark hair ornaments will not show up in dark hair but look terrific on blondes or redheads.

Combs, clips and slides are usually made of plastic and can be worn singly or in pairs. They are perfect for holding back fringes that are growing out, to pin up long hair and keep it off the neck, or to decorate short bobs. Many of them come in bright or pastel colours with an edging of shells, feathers or stones.

You don't need to stick to the conventional combs and clips when you are trying to dress up your hair. Try ribbons in bright prints, bandeau style scarves, large banana clips with animal skin patterns and even glittery chopsticks to hold up a topknot.

DETERMINE YOUR FACE SHAPE

The hairstyles that will best suit you will probably depend greatly on the shape of your face. The best way of determining your face shape is to measure it with a ruler. If you find this difficult, you can tie back your hair to keep it off your face, look into a mirror and draw the outline of your face directly onto the mirror itself. You can then take the dimensions of your face from this outline and use it to determine your face shape.

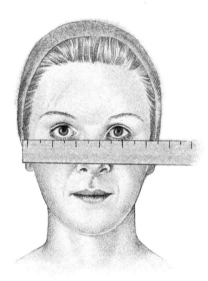

The first step is to determine whether your face is broad, long or average. To do this pin your hair back and then measure the widest part of your face which will usually be across the top of your cheekbones. The proportion of the length of your face compared to the width also affects the shape of your face. The classic oval face has a length equal to one and one half times its width. A round face is one that is almost as wide as it is broad, while a long face is one that is considerably longer from top to bottom than it is wide.

The next step is to measure from top to bottom. Look into a well-lit mirror and measure the length of your face from your hairline to the tip of your chin. In addition, study the width of your cheekbones, jawline and forehead as they also determine the shape of your face. A heart-shaped face is wider at the forehead and cheekbones than at the jaw. A square face has a broad forehead, wide cheekbones and a strong jawline, while a diamond-shaped face is wide at the cheeks with a narrow forehead and jaw.

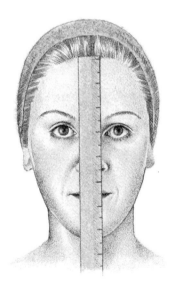

CHOOSING A HAIRSTYLE

When choosing a hairstyle the most important aspect to consider is whether or not it will suit your face shape. Your hair type will have also have considerable bearing on the style or cut that will work best for you. In addition, you must consider your height. If you are tall and large a short crop can make you appear larger still, while a huge shaggy mane on a petite woman can appear overpowering. Besides finding a style that will suit your face shape, body frame, and hair type, you want to choose a style that will flatter the features you want to emphasize and play down the features you wish to disguise. If you are uncertain about a style, ask your hairdresser for advice.

Short hair works best for round faces if it is cut to provide height and angles. Styles that are swept off the face or have lots of curls all over the head will simply emphasize your face's round shape. Pick a style with fullness at the crown and shorter sides, and avoid straight fringes. This style creates fullness around the top of the head while still retaining length behind the ears to provide more contour.

If your face is long, a style that adds width will suit you best. This could include curls or waves at the side, or a layered cut to add fullness. Avoid long straight hair, which accentuates a long face, as does a centre parting. This style provides width and movement with subtle asymmetry to reduce the appearance of length in the face.

Heart shaped faces are wide at the cheeks and forehead and narrow at the jaw. Avoid any styles that provide fullness at the cheeks. Sleek styles ending in shoulder length waves or short cuts with fullness on the crown will be the most flattering. This style, with its short, sharp shape and softness around the face complements the heart shaped face.

Square faces need softening up and a style that detracts from the angles. Gentle waves framing the face are ideal, such as a fringe and curls or waves around the ears. If your face is quite broad, avoid blunt cuts that finish on the jawline. This style provides length around the jaw and soft internal layering to soften the severity of the jaw.

An oval face is considered the perfect face shape that will suit almost any hairstyle. It is best to keep your style simple so that it doesn't detract from the balance of your features. Here a soft perm with detail around the face accentuates the cheekbones.

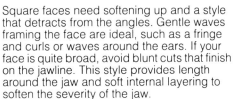

GETTING A GOOD CUT

The key to good looking hair is a good haircut. Hair should always be cut wet; it may be then retrimmed dry to correct any minor faults or irregularities. A good cut lasts about six to eight weeks, depending on the rate of your hair growth. Even if you are letting your hair grow, regular trims are essential. Hair grows unevenly and the shape of your cut will soon become ragged if left untrimmed. Regular trims also remove any damaged or split ends, keeping the hair in good condition.

Depending on the style hair is usually cut by one of two methods. A blunt cut styles the hair so that it is all the same length at any particular point of a hairstyle. This may be a short bob, a shoulder length fall, with or without a fringe. Blunt cuts look their best on straight hair, as the style stays in place more easily, but wavy hair can also look terrific if it is blunt cut and blow dried evenly.

A layered cut has many variations but the basic technique is the same. Layered hair is usually shorter on the top and sides and left longer at the back. It may also be cut very short around the back and sides. Layered hair can be used for any type of hair, but is especially good on very wavy or curly hair, bringing out the shape of the curl.

ALL ABOUT COLOURING

There are few women who have not experimented at least once with a change of hair colouring. Given the wide range of shades that can be achieved today, many have found a colour that they feel is right for them. This can be done with permanent tints, with semi-permanent colorants or with shampoo in products that add colour until the next wash. Bleaches are used to make the hair lighter.

Whether you want a radical change and a whole new image, or a subtle lift to your natural shade a professional colorist will be able to advise you on the shades that best suit your skin colouring. When you colour your hair, you must be prepared to change your makeup colours. And you must be ready for the necessary upkeep of your new hair colour so that it stays looking natural all the time.

Temporary rinses

Most temporary colorants work in conjunction with a shampoo washed into the hair or in a rinse that is applied after shampooing. These are the mildest form of hair coloring, and last only until the next shampoo. Because they only coat the surface of the hair with colour they are most effective on light hair and will make little difference to dark hair. And because they are the most predictable, they are ideal for women who want to experiment.

Semi-permanent colour

These colorants are usually shampooed into clean wet hair and left for 20–40 minutes before being rinsed out. The effect lasts from four to six shampoos. Some shades – red tones especially – are prone to rapid fading. Although these products are designed to penetrate the cuticle of the hair, they do not alter the natural pigmentation structure and are simply coating the cortex with colour. A major colour change cannot be achieved with these colorants, and they are used to intensify the color of your own hair or to lighten it by one or two shades. They are best on brown or dark shades, and should not be used on blonde hair. Some brands completely cover grey hair and, because they wash out gradually, there is no obvious regrowth line.

Vegetable dyes

Vegetable dyes are non-toxic and cannot harm your hair, but they are less easy to control than chemical dyes. Henna is probably the most commonly used vegetable dye. The henna powder is mixed with warm water until it has a pastelike consistency. The paste is applied to the hair and left for 30–60 minutes, rinsed out and the hair washed. Always use rubber gloves when applying henna or you will colour your hands as well as your hair. The results of henna on all shades of brown hair is excellent, but it makes blonde hair go orange. Other natural products can be used to give hair a lift. A final rinse of lemon juice after shampooing will bring out really pale highlights on naturally blonde hair, as will a rinse of camomile.

Permanent tints

These products actually change the structure of the hair to alter natural hair colour. These tints or dyes are mixed with hydrogen peroxide and penetrate the cortex of the hair to chemically change its colour composition. The new colour is permanent, although red shades are prone to fading. When new growth appears at the roots it will be necessary to have the colour retouched.

HAIR COLOURINGS

1 Auburn hair (natural)
2 Auburn (temporary colour)
3 Auburn (semi-permanent)
4 Auburn (henna)
5 Brown hair (henna)
6 Brown (semi-permanent)
7 Brown hair (natural)
8 Brown (temporary colour)
9 Blonde hair (natural)
10 Blonde (henna)
11 Blonde (permanent colour)
12 Blonde (temporary colour)
13 Brunette (natural)
14 Brunette (temporary colour)
15 Brunette (semi-permanent)
16 Brunette (henna)

Depending on the speed of growth, it may be necessary to retouch your hair after just three to four weeks to keep the colour looking natural and to avoid an obvious, harsh regrowth line.

Bleaching

To achieve pale blonde hair or to radically change natural hair colour some form of bleaching is usually necessary. Bleaching strips the hair of its natural pigmentation and another colour can then be substituted if desired. It works in a similar way to a permanent tint, but the volume of hydrogen peroxide used will be slightly greater. The exact strength of the solution and the amount of time needed for it to take effect will depend on the natural hair colour.

Bleaching makes the hair extremely dry and porous, so you should get professional advice before embarking on this. After bleaching you must be prepared to condition your hair after every shampoo and to have weekly deep conditioning treatments with oils.

Highlights and lowlights

There are alternative ways of changing your natural colour without going through the harsh bleaching process. Highlighting, streaking and tipping are especially good for blonde or light shades. The colour can be added to the tips of the hair only, or to individual sections around the sides and top of the face, as if the hair was lightened by the sun. On darker hair, lowlights can be added, in which a colour richer and darker than your natural shade is streaked into your hair.

In either of these a chemical lightener or darkener is added to small sections of the hair and left to work. The effect of highlights and lowlights is very natural as there is no hard line at the roots, and retouching is only needed every four to six months or so.

PERMANENT WAVING

If you know that you want a permanent curl or wave to your hair, the best way of achieving this is to have a permanent wave. Curling or setting only gives short term results that must be repeated every time you wash your hair.

How it works

A permanent is designed to actually rearrange the internal structure of the hair. By using a special solution that penetrates the hair shaft and breaks down its make up, the hair is left in a soft, almost plastic state. The hair structure is reformed by being wound around curlers or rollers, and then neutralized with a solution to hold the curl. The effect gradually wears off, although a perm usually holds its shape until the hair is cut off. The newer acid perms are very gentle on the hair, rarely cause frizz, and allow reperming at three or four month intervals.

As with setting, the size of the curl depends on the size of the rollers used. For a loose wave very fat rollers are used and a large amount of hair is wound around each roller. For a medium curl, the rollers are smaller and the perming solution is left on the hair for a little bit longer. Really tight curls are wound on tiny little rollers and the solution is left on the hair for quite a while.

Before you go ahead with a permanent, discuss it with your hairdresser. Perming hair that is already damaged or dry may cause it all to break off close to the scalp. A perm should never be used on a scalp that is inflamed or broken or sensitive to strong ingredients. The success of a perm depends to a large degree on the condition and quality of your hair. Hair that has been coloured is affected by perming too, and may lighten afterwards. If you want to perm and colour your hair, wait a week between processes to avoid damaging your hair, which may become very dry and brittle.

Types of perms

There are new types of permanents that are suitable for almost every type and length of hair. Some of the newer, more gentle perms are especially good for hair that has been coloured. Most of the differences of these new style perms depend on the type of rollers or rods that are used.

A body wave is good for short to medium-length layered or blunt-cut hair. As the name implies, it provides body and gentle waves to straight hair and can easily be blow dried smooth. The hair is wound on large perm rods for a full bodied look.

A flex perm is good for medium-length layered or long blunt-cut hair. The effect can range from fluffy curls to flowing waves. The hair is set on flexible rubber rods that are bent into different shapes to create a variety of effects.

A ladder perm is best for long blunt-cut hair. This type gives you a flowing cascade of waves. The hair is set on special curlers that are made of two rungs. The hair is woven between the rungs so the waves come out soft and even.

A root perm is good for hair of any length that is flat at the roots. It lifts the roots to give hair height and fullness. The perming solution is only applied to the roots of the hair and the bottom ends are protected with cling film. A root perm may need to be repeated more frequently than the other types to keep the effect constant.

Caring for permed hair

After having a perm your hair will be much drier. You will need to condition your hair after every shampoo, and use a conditioning oil treatment once a week. Avoid overbrushing or blowdrying for at least a week after the perm as the heat may cause the hair to snap and split. Avoid heated tongs and rollers for the same reason. For maximum curl, leave your hair to dry naturally after washing and conditioning.

HAIR PROBLEMS

Most hair problems have more to to with the way the hair and scalp are treated than your general health (see chart below). It is important to eat well, and get regular exercise as this improves the circulation to the scalp and may relieve dandruff and scalp problems. The major causes of hair problems are using harsh hair products, overprocessing treatments such as perms, colouring and bleaching, and overheating from the sun, blowdrying or heated rollers.

To maintain the health and condition of your hair, you should treat any problems as soon as they occur. If you are unsure about the cause, consult your doctor, who may refer you to a dermatologist or a trichologist (a doctor specializing in hair and scalp problems). The most common hair problems are dandruff, hair loss, grey hair and split ends.

COMMON HAIR PROBLEMS		
Problem	**Cause**	**Treatment**
Dandruff	Dandruff is a build up of dry dead skin cells that are shed naturally. It is usually associated with dry skin and hair but can also occur in people with oily skin.	Try a specially formulated dandruff shampoo. If this doesn't help, consult your doctor who may be able to prescribe something stronger. Do not use strong dandruff shampoos more than once a week or so, as they may irritate the scalp.
Hair loss	Hair is shed as part of its growing cycle, but excessive hair loss could be a sign of illness, stress or simply age. Hair loss is also quite common after pregnancy. Bald patches, known as alopecia, are a different condition. In this case the hair comes out in clumps and leaves small bald patches on the scalp.	If you notice hair loss, consult your doctor who may refer you to a dermatologist or a trichologist (a hair and scalp specialist). Hair loss after pregnancy usually reverses and should be no cause for concern. Some cases of alopecia can be treated, but in others the hair loss is permanent.
Grey hair	Grey hair is actually white, since white hair mixed with dark hair gives the impression of being grey. Grey hair has no colour pigment in the cortex. Most people notice the odd grey hair in their 20s or 30s. Sudden shock, illness or stress may bring this process forward.	There is no treatment to stop the loss of colour pigment. Grey hair can be coloured to blend in with the rest of the hair.
Split ends	Probably the most common hair complaint, split ends usually occur in dry hair as the result of rough treatment.	Early signs of drying and splitting should be treated with conditioners and hot oil treatments. Have ends trimmed regularly to avoid the split travelling up the hair shaft.

HAND &
FOOT CARE

Most women tend to ignore their hands and feet when performing their beauty routines and only give them attention when they become troublesome. Although little can be done about changing the basic structure and shape of your hands and feet, you can easily make them better looking by lavishing some regular care and attention on them. Having attractive, cared for hands and feet is an integral part of good grooming, and can make all the difference in the world.

HAND CARE

Your hands are one of your most expressive features. They are one of the first things that people notice about you and attractive, healthy hands are an indication that you take care of yourself. Few of us have the long slim hands we might like but it is possible for every woman to have better looking hands by giving them a little attention. This includes regular maintenance of the nails and cuticles, applying hand cream to keep the skin soft and smooth, and making sure that nail polish is never chipped or cracked.

There is little you can do about the shape of your hands but you can do a lot to improve the condition of your nails. The visible part of your nails is, in fact, dead keratin, a hard enamel-like substance. The only living part of the nail is the matrix, which lies at the base of the nail bed. This is where the nail cells grow and push forward. In some women the top of the matrix is visible as the half moon.

The nail bed is protected by a thin strip of skin around the nail plate, known as the cuticle. Healthy cuticles should be pale and pink in colour, and should stand slightly away from the nail. Neglected cuticles lack elasticity, feel dry and tough, and become stuck to the surface of the nail. Nails grow slowly, about 1.5 mm a month, and take about three months to grow from the root to the tip; they grow twice as quickly if you bite them.

THE BASICS

Your hands take a lot of punishment every day; they are immersed in water, covered with soaps and cleansing solutions, and perform a wide variety of tasks, all which can affect the condition of your hands and nails.

To keep your hands looking good, you should always protect them when doing housework. Wear rubber gloves when doing dishes or using cleaning products, and wear gardening gloves when working outdoors. And always wear gloves in cold weather to keep your hands warm and help improve circulation. Dry your hands thoroughly after they have been in water, since the longer water is on the skin the more dehydrating it is.

Apply lots of rich moisturizing cream after washing and drying your hands, the more the better. The best way to get into the habit is to keep some hand cream in almost every room of the house so it will be within easy reach. To keep the cuticles in good condition push them back gently after a bath or shower when the skin is soft, and massage in cuticle cream nightly. Don't continuously pick at or push your cuticles or you may damage the matrix and cause ridges, spots and lines in the nails.

THE PERFECT MANICURE

To keep your hands looking good, a weekly manicure is an essential. If you want to do a professional job it is important to have the right equipment. You will need:

- Emery boards
- Nail scissors or clippers
- Orange sticks and rubber-tipped hoof sticks
- Cuticle cream
- Cuticle remover
- Nail polish remover
- Cotton wool balls
- Chamois buffers and buffing cream
- A bowl of warm soapy water

The first steps
Before you begin, assemble all the equipment you will need. Then remove all traces of nail polish with polish remover. Soak a cotton wool ball in the remover and rub it gently across the nails, working from the cuticle to the tip of the nail.

The next step is to file the nails with an emery board. An emery board has two surfaces, a roughened side to do the filing and smoother side for finishing off. Use the smoother side and file the nails in one direction working towards the centre. Hold the emery board by the narrow end, and don't use a back and forth sawing movement. Avoid filing too low down at the sides of the nails as this will weaken them and cause them to split.

Cuticle care
Once your nails are neatly filed, you should start on the cuticles. Apply a small amount of a good cuticle cream to each nail bed, massaging it in. Using a rubber-tipped hoof stick, gently loosen the skin all around the nail, then soak the hands in a bowl of warm water for a few minutes. When the cuticles have softened, gently scrub the nails and cuticles using a soft nail brush. Rinse well in clean water and dry. Push the cuticles back again with the hoof stick and apply hand cream, massaging it over the fingers, hands and wrists.

Use cuticle clippers to remove hangnails or torn skin, and apply cuticle remover around the cuticle, working it in with the hoof stick. Cuticle removers do not actually remove the skin; instead they help to loosen the

Emery boards, pumice stones, cuticle clippers and hoof sticks can help you have well groomed hands and feet (overleaf).

60 MINUTE MANICURE

Your hands are one of the first things that people notice about you. Regardless of their shape, it is easy to have attractive hands with a little care and a weekly manicure.

▲ File your nails in one direction, from the outside towards the centre. Do not saw back and forth.

▲ Massage in cuticle cream and push the cuticles back. Soak hands in warm water and then brush the nails.

▲ Apply cuticle remover and leave it on for the specified time. Push back the cuticles with a hoof stick and then rinse the nails in clean water.

▲ You can buff your nails to make them shine. Always buff in one direction, usually from the nail bed to the tip.

◄ Apply polish using three strokes, one down the centre of the nail, with one either side. Be sure and let each coat dry well.

▲ To exercise your hands, tightly clench your fists. Unclench quickly and stretch your fingers as wide as you can ten times.

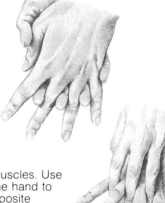

▲ A hand massage relaxes muscles. Use the thumb and forefinger of one hand to massage the fingers of the opposite hand, working from the fingertip to the base. Massage between each finger, then massage each knuckle.

cuticle and remove any acid deposits underneath. Leave the cuticle remover on the hands for the stipulated period of time, then immerse the fingertips in warm water and clean and brush the nails. Clean the suface of each nail again very throughly with a cotton wool ball dampened with polish remover. This will remove all traces of soap and creams or oils. It also prepares the nail surface for the basecoat and ensures that polish will adhere properly.

Mending broken nails

At this point, mend any nails that are cracked or splitting; this should only be done if you are planning to polish the nails, as the patch will show on bare nails. Patching kits include a small sheet of fibrous tissue, plus a special fixative that holds the patch firmly in place. Tear the paper so that the edges are jagged, hold the patch over the forefinger and apply the adhesive. Then place the patch over the split; use tweezers if it makes positioning the patch easier. Put a drop of polish remover on your forefinger and smooth over the patch. Then press the patch down and wrap it under the nail tip. When the patch is smooth, apply a coat of adhesive over it, then polish as usual.

Buffing

If you are not wearing polish, this is the time to buff the nails. Work the chamois buffer in one direction, usually from the nail bed to the tip. This improves the blood circulation and makes the nails shine. There are also special buffing creams that you can use with the buffer.

Polishing

The first step in polishing is to apply basecoat, which protects the nail from becoming stained by brightly coloured polish and helps prevent polish from chipping. Only three strokes of polish are needed if your nails are to look neat. The first should be down the centre of the nail from the base to the tip, and then one stroke in the same direction on either side of the first.

Most polishes develop their true colour after two or three coats, although there are specially formulated single coat polishes available. Be sure to allow the polish to dry thoroughly between coats. There are special sprays and fixatives to help polish dry quicker, and some of the newer brands are made to be quick-drying, which comes in handy when you are in a bit of a rush. To finish your manicure, apply a topcoat to help seal the polish.

False nails

Stick-on false nails are the easiest type to apply at home, and there are a number of different kits that come equipped with a set of nails and a tube of adhesive. The procedure varies from brand to brand, so always follow the manufacturer's instructions. Be sure and choose nails that closely match the size of your own. You may need to trim or file false nails before using to get them the proper size and shape.

If you want really long nails, nail extensions are usually the answer. They are difficult to apply correctly at home, and you should get a professional to do the job; a number of beauty salons provide this service. The process is time consuming, though, and may prove expensive.

HAND AND NAIL PROBLEMS

A number of disorders can affect the hands and many of them can be prevented (see chart below). One of the most common problems is eczema, which is an inflammation of the horny layers of the skin. Other skin problems include calluses, warts, chilblains, and whitlows.

Your nails are also prone to various disorders, and can be an indication of your health and general well-being. Stress or tension can cause thinning, ridging or furrowing in the nails. The nails may develop ridges if there is a circulatory problem, and pallid nails are often a sign of anemia.

COMMON HAND PROBLEMS		
Problem	**Cause**	**Treatment**
Chapped skin	Chapping is usually caused by the skin drying out. It is often worse in cold weather.	Moisturize the hands regularly or use a barrier cream. Keep your hands out of water. Wear rubber gloves for washing up or when cleaning with detergents, and wear warm gloves when outside in cold weather.
Chilblains	These small painful itchy swellings are caused by a combination of poor circulation and cold weather.	Wear gloves when outside and try not to expose your hands to very extreme temperature changes. If you smoke you should stop, as this inhibits circulation.
Eczema	The predisposition to eczema is inherited. An attack can be triggered off by a decline in general health or stress. It may also be triggered by an allergic reaction to a specific substance.	Your doctor can prescribe creams or tablets to ease the symptoms of eczema. When the condition is bad, avoid contact with soap and water. Apply emollient creams often during the day.
Whitlow	This infection of the nail fold is caused by the entry of bacteria into the skin around the nail.	Whitlows are usually self-curing but can be painful. If severe you may need to have professional treatment. The whitlow may need to be opened under local anaesthetic.

Nail polish comes in a wide range of colours, from bright glossy reds to pale pinks and neutrals (left).

FOOT CARE

It is important to give your feet the best care you can since they are responsible for taking the weight of the entire body, for maintaining balance, and for facilitating movement. They also get a lot of exercise; the average person takes about 15,000 steps a day, or about 70,000 miles in a lifetime.

Almost everybody is born with perfect feet, but by the time they reach adulthood about four out of five people have developed some kind of foot problem. Most of these are due to lack of care or wearing the wrong shoes. Daily washing, a weekly pedicure, and wearing proper shoes will ensure that your feet will look their best and will help to prevent any problems developing that may later cause considerable pain and discomfort.

THE BASICS

To maintain the health of your feet you should wash them every day and scrub the nails with a soft nail brush. Always dry the feet thoroughly, paying special attention to the area between the toes. After drying, apply a moisturizing cream or talc.

If you have a problem with foot odour you may need to wash your feet more often. There are also special antiperspirants and talcs on the market to treat the problem, as well as special deodorized insoles that you can put in your shoes.

Check the condition of your feet daily, and immediately treat any corns, blisters or bunions that you find. If you have any problems or worries, consult your doctor or a chiropodist, who is a doctor that specializes in treating foot problems.

Try and sit with your feet elevated for a short time each day and, if possible, walk around barefoot as much as you can to let your feet breathe. To improve the circulation, keep your feet warm with socks and boots in the winter, wear socks and stockings made of natural fibres, and change your footwear daily. It is also important to buy shoes that fit and if you wear high heels, change the height of your heels at least once a day to avoid any problems developing.

If you have been standing or walking for a long period of time, your feet may be sore and ache. To help relieve this, give yourself a footbath. Dissolve 1 cup of Epsom salts or baking soda in warm water. Soak your feet for about 15 minutes, then dry them thoroughly.

You should exercise your feet regularly to keep them limber and supple. This is especially important if you often wear high heels. It only takes a few minutes, and can be done almost anywhere.

First, stand barefoot with your feet together. Raise yourself up on the balls of your feet slowly, then lower yourself slowly. Repeat this ten times. Sit on a chair with your legs stretched out in front of you and your feet raised from the floor. Move your feet up and down, working from the ankles. Another good exercise to strengthen the muscles in the feet is to practice picking up a pencil with your toes.

Massage also helps to soothe sore and tired feet by improving the circulation, and can relax tense or tight muscles. Apply a liberal amount of cream to the feet, and start by massaging the ball of the foot with both hands using firm, circular movements. Then massage the instep and the heel. Press each toe firmly between the thumb and forefinger of one hand, then press firmly between the bones at the base of the foot, again using the thumb and forefinger. Clasp your toes with your hand and bend them towards you. Then release them and repeat. Use both hands to pull each toe gently away from the one next to it.

THE PERFECT PEDICURE

During the summer your feet are usually on show, and most women give themselves a pedicure so that neat, polished nails peep out from their sandals. But just because your feet are hidden away for the rest of the year doesn't mean they should be neglected.

A weekly pedicure year-round will keep your feet looking their best. The ideal time for this is after a bath, as the skin on the feet is already softened. If you give yourself a pedicure at another time, be sure and soak the feet for a few minutes.

The first steps

Remove any polish with cotton wool soaked in polish remover. Cut your toenails with proper clippers rather than scissors, and cut the toenails straight across rather than into the sides; this will avoid ingrowing toenails and prevent the nails from digging into the skin on the surrounding toes. Don't cut toenails too short; try to leave a rim of white at the edge. Once nails are cut to the proper length, file them lightly with an emery board. Then massage in a little cuticle cream to soften the skin in the area.

Removing hard skin

Soak your feet in a bowl of warm water and scrub the toes with a soft nail brush. Dry the toes and feet thoroughly and then use a pumice stone or special rough skin scraper to get rid of any hard skin, which usually develops on the heels and the balls of the feet. There are new liquid hard skin removers on the market that are applied to dry skin and then gently rubbed off, taking the hard skin with it; these are also good for removing dead skin on the top of the feet and around the ankles. Then rinse the feet in clean water and dry them thoroughly.

HAND AND FOOT CARE

30 MINUTE PEDICURE

There is no reason to neglect your feet just because they are hidden away. The proper shoes and a weekly pedicure will keep them looking and feeling their best.

◄ Wash your feet every day and scrub your nails with a soft nail brush. If you notice any problems have them treated immediately.

► Always dry your feet thoroughly after washing. Pay special attention to the area between the toes to avoid any infection.

▲ Clip your nails straight across. File them lightly with an emery board and massage in cuticle cream.

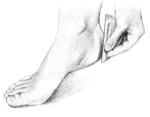

▲ Areas of hard skin usually appear on the heels or the balls of the feet. Remove them with a pumice stone or special callus remover, then rinse in clean water and dry.

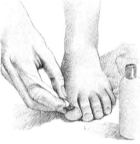

▲ Apply cuticle remover to the nails. Gently push back the cuticles with a hoof stick to loosen the skin from the nail surface.

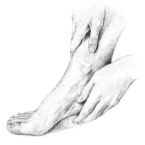

▲ Rinse and dry the feet and massage in cream. You can then buff or polish your toenails as you would your fingernails.

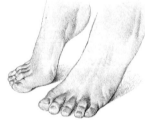

▲ To exercise feet, raise up and down on the balls of feet or stand on some books, grip the edges, and release.

72

The final stages

Push the cuticles back gently with a towel. Apply cuticle remover and leave it on for the required time. Use a hoof stick to push the cuticles back gently and loosen the cuticle from the nail surface. When all this is completed, massage a rich moisturizing cream into the feet, concentrating on the areas where the rough skin builds up. If you are applying polish, wipe over each nail with polish remover to prepare it for the basecoat.

Apply polish to the toenails in the same way you would to the fingernails. Use three strokes, with the first going down the centre, and then one on each side. To avoid smudging it helps to use one of the specially designed sponge pieces to keep the toes separated while the polish is drying. Allow time for the polish to dry, then apply a topcoat or sealer.

If you prefer the natural look, you can buff toenails instead. Buff in one direction, preferably from the base to the tip, and don't rub too hard or the nails will get hot.

FOOT PROBLEMS

Most foot problems are caused by ill-fitting shoes, and it is important to buy ones that fit properly. When trying on shoes, make sure they do not rub against the big toe or cut into the side or back of the ankle. They should fit snugly across the widest part of the feet without pinching, and should not push the toes into each other. Loose shoes can cause problems as much as tight shoes can, so make sure that yours are the correct size. When trying on shoes, wear the socks or stockings that you will be wearing with the shoes to ensure a proper fit. Do not try on shoes when you are hot or when you have been walking as your feet may be swollen – shoes you buy at these times often feel too loose the following morning. If you are flat footed, you may need to buy arch supports for extra comfort and support.

It is a good idea to have your feet measured professionally every once in awhile. Your feet may change size occasionally, and shoe sizes vary from one manufacturer to another. Always try on both the left and right shoes, as most people have one foot that is larger than the other. If the difference is great, buy the larger size and have an insole put into the other. Be sure and stand up and walk around in the shoes before you buy them. A shoe that is comfortable when you are sitting down is not an indication that it is the correct size.

If you notice any problem developing on your feet, have it checked and treated immediately. Most of the more common foot problems are minor but may become very painful if left untreated for too long.

The most common foot problems are corns, calluses, bunions, ingrowing toenails and infections such as athlete's foot. Some of these can be successfully treated at home, while others may require professional help (see chart on page 74).

COMMON FOOT PROBLEMS		
Problem	**Cause**	**Treatment**
Athlete's foot	This fungal infection causes scaling, peeling, itchy skin between the toes. Athlete's foot is contagious, and thrives in warm damp areas.	Be sure and dry your feet thoroughly after washing, particularly between the toes. Apply an antifungal cream or powder twice a day. If the condition does not clear up, consult your doctor.
Bunion	Bunions are a deformity of the joint between the big toe and the foot. They are usually due to tight-fitting shoes putting severe pressure on the area around the big toe, causing the toe to bend inwards against the other toes. A bunion may become painful, swollen and tender.	Wear properly-fitting shoes, and wear a bunion shield on the affected area. If the bunion is very painful, see your doctor who may refer you to a chiropodist. If the bunion is left untreated and becomes severe, surgery may later be required to remove part of the bone.
Callus	Calluses are areas of hard skin that build up due to pressure from new or ill-fitting shoes.	A pumice stone can be used to remove the callus, and there are also special callus removers. If you cannot treat it at home, a chiropodist will be able to remove it for you.
Corn	Similar to a callus, corns are localized areas of hard dead skin that build up due to friction and pressure. They can be caused by loose-fitting shoes as well as tight shoes. The skin responds to friction by producing a protective layer of dead cells. These cells then pile up, become thick and form a corn.	Do not use a home treatment to remove corns, as these preparations do not always limit themselves to the area you want treated; this can cause infection. See a chiropodist, who will be able to cut the corn away.
Ingrowing toenail	The underlying cause of an ingrowing toenail is usually a very fleshy toe pad into which the nail can sink and bite.	Most can be treated by a chiropodist. Regular visits every eight weeks or so may be necessary.
Vorruca	Often mistaken for a corn, a verruca is an inverted wart that grows into the skin, often in the sole of the foot. They are caused by a virus and are usually picked up in public places where the feet are bare, such as swimming pools.	Some verrucas disappear without any treatment while others stay and become painful. Consult your doctor or see a chiropodist, who may freeze the verruca to kill the area of skin that the verruca lives in.

BODY CARE

BODY CARE

It is not just the parts of your body that are seen, like your hair and face, that need looking after. The rest of your body, too, deserves regular maintenance if you are to feel clean and healthy. A number of these beauty routines are performed daily, such as bathing or brushing your teeth. Others can be performed once in awhile, such as exfoliating your skin or removing unwanted hair. Caring for your body from top to toe creates endless rewards. You will look better, feel better, and be confident that you are always looking the best you can.

PERSONAL CLEANLINESS

To feel clean you also need to smell clean. Sweat itself does not smell, but when it remains on the skin for awhile the body's natural bacteria makes it decompose, causing odour. These bacteria flourish in warm damp surroundings – in the areas where sweat is trapped by clothing.

To eliminate unpleasant body odour it is important to remove sweat before it has a chance to decompose. For most people this means having a daily bath or shower; using an underarm deodorant or antiperspirant prevents sweating and cuts down odours. In addition, you should wash and change your clothes regularly. Sweat clings to fabric, especially synthetics. Wear loose-fitting clothes in natural fabrics, which will allow sweat to evaporate.

Bathing

For your daily bath or shower a mild soap and a clean sponge or flannel are all that you need to keep fresh. Don't use antibacterial or deodorizing soaps, which will upset your body's natural cleansing mechanism. Although many people are used to taking baths, a shower is probably a better way of getting clean, as you are rinsing off in clean water. Also, a shower can be invigorating as the pressure of the water helps to speed up the circulation.

No matter whether you take a bath or a shower, make sure that the water is warm but not too hot; hot water will make you sweat and can dry out the skin. Never remain in the bath or shower for so long that your skin becomes wrinkled. The longer that you are immersed in water the more natural oil that is lost and the more dehydrated your skin becomes.

Deodorants and antiperspirants

These products offer extra protection for the underarm area. Deodorants do not stop perspiration, they only stop the bacteria in sweaty areas from decomposing the sweat. If you perspire heavily, use an antiperspirant, which dehydrates the sweat glands so that less sweat is produced.

Both of these products come in a variety of forms, such as creams, sticks, roll-ons and aerosol sprays. Roll-ons are probably better than aerosols as they are generally more effective and they go exactly where you need them to. Experiment to find a brand you like, and use it regularly. Never use them on inflamed or broken skin, or immediately after shaving under your arms; apply them at least a half hour before shaving. If you get any adverse reaction, change your product immediately.

Feminine hygiene

There is no need to use special feminine hygiene sprays or products in the vaginal area; soap and water are all that is needed to keep the genitals clean. The vagina itself is self-cleansing, and the deodorant sprays and scented sanitary protection products that are available can upset the delicate balance of its natural secretions, causing irritations or allergies. The vagina only smells unpleasant if some infection is present. If you do notice an odour, consult your doctor who will be able to determine the cause.

DENTAL CARE

Maintaining the hygiene of your teeth and gums is an important part of your health care. Since you only have one set of teeth as an adult, taking the best care of them you can avoids the possibility of serious dental problems arising later. Good dental care includes daily brushing and flossing and regular check-ups at the dentist.

Regular brushing and flossing prevents the build up of plaque, the great enemy of teeth and gums. This sticky film that forms on teeth is made up of saliva and soft material that is formed from the saliva and bacterial cells themselves. Plaque formation is encouraged by eating or drinking sweet or starchy food. Plaque starts off soft but eventually hardens, forming a coating on the teeth around the gum margin. This build up can damage the tooth enamel and encourage tooth decay. Plaque also irritates and erodes the gum margin, causing gum disease.

You should have twice yearly check-ups at the dentist so that your teeth can be examined for signs of any problems; they can then be treated before they become serious. At the check-up your dentist will also clean your teeth by descaling them and removing any calcium deposits from the gum, which helps to prevent gum disease.

Toothbrushes and toothpastes

It is important to choose the right toothbrush to get the maximum benefit from it. A nylon brush is preferable to bristle, as bristle splits and loses its shape quickly. Choose a brush with a small head so that you can easily clean the back teeth. A soft or medium bristle brush is best, as the harder brushes may damage the tooth enamel and the gums. Change your toothbrush regularly, about every month or so, as the bristles soon get soft.

Having a bath, using deodorant and brushing and flossing teeth should be part of every woman's daily beauty routine (overleaf).

BODY CARE

There is a wide variety of toothpastes on the market. Some contain fluoride, which helps protect against tooth decay, and the newer ones go some way to preventing plaque. Others have special ingredients for freshening the breath, for removing nicotine stains from the teeth of smokers, or are specifically for people with sensitive teeth. Choosing a toothpaste is often a matter of taste. When you find one you prefer, continue to use it regularly to prevent tooth decay.

Brushing

It is important to clean your teeth after every meal to remove food particles and prevent the build-up of plaque. Thorough cleaning helps to keep the breath fresh, as decomposing food can cause bad breath. Brushing helps to massage the gums, keeping them in good condition.

To brush properly, apply a small amount of toothpaste to your brush. Place your brush against your teeth at a 45 degree angle and gently brush from the gum margin upwards or downwards, depending on if you are brushing your upper or lower teeth. Be sure and clean the inner surfaces of the teeth, the back teeth, and the tongue. Don't press too hard, and don't push the brush down into the gums. To check on your efficiency, use a disclosing rinse after brushing, which colours any remaining plaque a bright pink.

Flossing

Dental floss should be used at least once a day to clean between the teeth. It should be used delicately so as to not damage the gums. Unwaxed dental floss is probably more effective than waxed, but if you have a lot of fillings or uneven edges it may catch on the teeth; used waxed instead.

To floss, wind a short length of floss around the second fingers of each hand. Slide it gently down between each of the teeth, taking care to press it against the side of the tooth. Then gently slide it upwards out of the teeth, removing any food particles with it. Repeat until you have flossed between all of the teeth. Use a new length of floss if it snags or tears.

You can also use soft wooden toothpicks to gently rub the gum margins between the teeth; this helps to keep the gums firm and healthy.

Bad breath

The usual causes of bad breath are eating, drinking, smoking, and tooth or gum decay. If you are brushing and flossing regularly and suffer from bad breath, see your dentist to eliminate the possibility of any gum disease. If you smoke you should stop or learn to live with smoker's breath. Remember, too, that certain foods can make your breath smell long after you have eaten them.

There is no need to use mouthwashes to try and mask bad breath as they are not very effective and the feeling of freshness only lasts about 15 minutes. Regular use of mouthwashes may upset the delicate balance of the bacteria in the mouth and eventually do more harm than good.

SMART SUNBATHING

Few people understand the damage that excessive sunbathing can cause. A lightly tanned skin can look attractive, but it may be at the expense of the health of your skin. The sun robs your skin of valuable moisture, dehydrating it, and in extreme cases can cause skin cancer. Sunbathing is ageing as it breaks down collagen and speeds up the development of wrinkles.

The sun changes your skin colour because a pigment called melanin is produced as a defence mechanism against the ultraviolet rays. The more melanin that is made, the darker your skin will turn. How quickly and easily you tan depends on your natural melanin concentration. The sun also stimulates the skin to undergo malignant change, which encourages skin cancer. Although it takes many years of exposure to the sun to trigger this, the fairer you are the more susceptible your skin.

Sun protection

If you are determined to sunbathe, it is important to follow some guidelines to protect your skin. Regardless of your skin type, always use a sunscreen. The degree to which a product screens out the sun's burning rays is called the "protection factor". Follow the manufacturer's guidelines in choosing one that is suitable for you. If you are in doubt, use a higher protection factor until you see how your skin reacts. The higher the protection factor, the more efficient the sunscreen. Apply it often, and always reapply after swimming as most sunscreens are not waterproof. You may want to use a sunblock on very sensitive areas, such as the nose and lips, to eliminate any chance of burning.

The fairer your skin the more likely it is to burn, so know your limit. Even dark skins reach a point at which they will not get any darker. Remember, there is no cure for sunburn. Start out slowly, staying out in the sun for just 10 to 30 minutes a day until your skin has developed a little colour. Work up to longer periods, adding 15 minutes each day. Avoid sunbathing during the hottest time of the day, from midday until 2pm, when ultraviolet radiation is at its most intense.

Sunbeds

These treatments simulate the sun's natural ultraviolet rays to help you achieve an all over tan. They may be helpful to prepare your skin before a holiday in the sun, but should be used wisely and with care.

Time yourself carefully, since you burn just as you would in natural sunlight. Build up your tan slowly; it may take several sessions before you notice any colour change. Always wear goggles to protect your eyes when under a sunbed.

Some of the manufacturers of the newer sunbeds claim that you can tan without burning and without damaging the skin. Although you may not burn you are still doing permanent damage to the deeper layers of the skin.

BATHING BEAUTY

Make the most of your bath by giving yourself a special beauty treatment at the same time. The steam from a warm bath will help face or hair conditioning treatments work, and the warm water will soften the skin on your hands and feet, preparing them for a manicure or pedicure.

Bath additives

Commercial bath products can be added to the water to soften and moisturize the skin. Bath salts and crystals soften the water as well as scent it, but can dry out your skin. Bubble baths foam up with water, making the bath rich and luxurious. They are usually detergent based, and should not be used for dry skin unless there are special moisturizers added. Bath gels clean your skin as well as soften the water. They, too, are detergent based and may be too harsh for dry skin.

Bath milks are ideal for dry skin, as they soften the water and contain no harsh ingredients. It you have oily skin, avoid bath milks as they may make the condition worse. Bath oils protect dry skin from the dehydrating effects of the water by coating the skin in a fine film of oil.

Special baths

In addition to cleaning, baths can also relax, soothe and invigorate, depending on what is added to the water. Try using herbs, such as camomile, mint, elderflowers or rosemary. Just tie the herbs in a muslin bag, hang the bag from the hot water tap and let the herbs infuse into the bathwater.

A milk bath is good for soothing dry skin. Add one pint of milk (or one cup of powdered milk) to the water. Add a few drops of clear honey or rose oil to scent the bath as well.

Oatmeal helps to exfoliate the skin and is an excellent soap substitute. Fill a muslin bag with a handful of rolled oats and use it to scrub the skin.

Body scrubs

Exfoliation helps to keep the skin on the body smooth and soft by removing the top layer of dead skin cells. The massaging action also helps to stimulate the circulation, improving skin tone. Concentrate on the problem areas, which are usually the upper arms, thighs, buttocks, heels and elbows. A number of exfoliating products are on the market; some are grainy creams that you rub on dampened skin, others are rough-textured mitts or sponges to be used in the bath.

After exfoliating, always apply a body lotion or moisturizer as soon as you have dried yourself and while your skin is still warm. None of the exfoliating products should be used daily; once or twice a week is usually enough. Never use exfoliating agents on sensitive or dry skin, skin that is broken or inflamed, or if you have acne.

Bath additives come in a wide range of forms, such as crystals, grains, oils and creams (overleaf).

20 MINUTE BODY CARE

Body care starts with personal cleanliness. Use your daily bathtime to perform some additional beauty routines to keep your body smooth and fresh from head to toe.

▶ To remove rough skin on elbows use one of the special rough skin removers. These lotions are applied before bathing while the skin is still dry. Gently massage the area with the lotion to rub away the dead skin. Rinse off the excess lotion in the bath or shower.

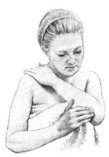

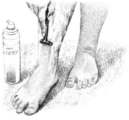

▲ If you shave your legs the best time is before you have a bath or shower so you can wash off any excess shaving cream. Always shave against the direction of the hair growth using long smooth strokes, being careful around the ankles and knees to avoid any cuts or nicks.

▶ While in the bath use a friction mitt to exfoliate and stimulate circulation. Wet mitt thoroughly and rub gently.

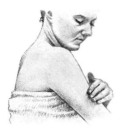

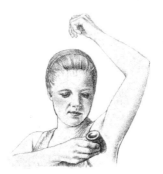

▲ Always apply lots of body cream or moisturizer after a bath, particularly after exfoliating. Pay special attention to those areas that are driest

◀ Finally, use a deodorant or antiperspirant every day to reduce sweating and body odour. Never apply either after shaving the underarms as it will irritate and inflame the skin; wait at least half an hour.

BODY CARE

HAIR REMOVAL

Hair grows naturally all over the body, except for the palms and the soles of the feet. Unwanted hair can be a problem for many women, especially if it is on the chin and upper lip. In addition, many women like to remove the hair from their underarms and legs. There are several methods for removing unwanted hair. Some are short term, such as shaving and plucking, while other methods like waxing last quite a while longer. Electrolysis is the only permanent method of hair removal.

It is important to determine what method of hair removal will be most effective for the different areas of your body (see chart opposite), as some methods are much better suited to a particular part of the body than others.

Plucking

Plucking is the easiest and safest way to remove stray hairs from your face, breast or abdomen. Using eyebrow tweezers, pluck out the hair by its root. The hair will grow back again but will not be any coarser or thicker. Apply astringent before plucking to reduce discomfort, and never pluck a hair from a mole or wart.

Shaving

One of the quickest, easiest and cheapest methods of removing unwanted hair from legs and underarms is shaving. Because the hair has been cut the blunt end can feel coarse. Regrowth appears within a few days, so you will need to shave regularly to keep skin soft and smooth. For best results, shave when your hair is wet as it will be softer, or use shaving cream. Shave against the direction of hair growth. If you are shaving your bikini line, use a razor specially designed for that area. Be sure and moisturize the skin after.

Depilation

The chemicals in depilatories dissolve unwanted hair, giving a smoother and longer-lasting result than shaving. Depilatories, which are available as creams, gels or sprays, are applied to the skin, left on for the required amount of time, then washed off. They can be messy to use, they have a strong smell and can irritate the skin. Try a patch test first, to make sure your skin will not react to the chemicals.

Bleaching

This is an excellent way to conceal dark hair on delicate areas or for smaller areas, such as the upper lip and chin. Bleaching is inexpensive and easy, and the results last about a month, until the darker roots grow out. The preparation is applied to the hair, left on for the required amount of time, then rinsed away. It is painless and harmless, but again a patch test should be tried before bleaching a larger area.

Waxing

Effective and long lasting, waxing is most often used for the legs and bikini line. Regrowth does not appear for about a month, but the drawback is that hair must grow to about ¼ inch before it can be waxed. Usually carried out in a salon, heated wax or wax strips are applied to the skin; when the wax is removed the hair is comes away with it. As waxing pulls the hair out by the roots, the skin is smooth and new hair is softer to the touch. It can be painful, though, and the skin may be irritated for about a day.

Electrolysis

This is the only method of permanent hair removal. A fine wire needle is inserted into the hair follicle and an electric current is passed through it to kill the hair root. Electrolysis must be performed by a professional. The process can be painful, time consuming and expensive, and is best for small areas of unwanted hair such as the upper lip and chin. The finer hairs in these areas may require only one electrolysis session but the coarser hairs may need several. They will grow progressively finer after each treatment until they disappear altogether.

HAIR REMOVAL METHODS

	Plucking	Shaving	Waxing	Bleaching	Depilation	Electrolysis
Upper lip	•			•	•	•
Chin	•			•	•	•
Eyebrows	•					•
Nipples	•			•	•	•
Underarms		•	•		•	
Abdomen	•		•		•	•
Bikini area		•	•		•	•
Legs		•	•		•	

MAKES SCENTS

The same fragrance never smells the same on two women and can differ as the result of many factors, such as the weather and body temperature. The warmer your skin, the more scent it will send into the air. Skin colour, too, can make a difference as dark skin tends to maintain a higher temperature than light skin. Different skin types take to different types of fragrance. If you have oily skin, your natural oils makes fragrance more potent and longer lasting, while dry skin rapidly soaks up anything you put on it and fragrance fades quickly. Fragrance is also affected by smoking, which reduces its staying power, as can internal or external medication.

Scent comes in different strengths. Perfume, which is the strongest, is also the most expensive form of fragrance. It lasts for about four to six hours. Parfum de toilette, which contains more alcohol than perfume, its not as strong smelling as perfume and lasts for about five hours. Eau de toilette has more water and alcohol than perfume. It is much lighter than either perfume or eau de toilette, and can be applied more liberally. It lasts about two to four hours. Eau de cologne is the least strong of the three. It is much lighter in oils and less costly than either perfume or toilet water, and lasts about two hours.

Most fragrances now come in a range of associated products, including bath soaps, body lotions, talcs, bath oils and even deodorant. Using products in the same fragrance as your scent, called layering, intensifies the fragrance and helps it to stay with you longer. It also means you need to use less perfume or cologne, and will avoid the problem of your scent clashing with other products you use on your skin.

Choosing a scent

The best time to shop for a scent is in the late afternoon or evening, when your sense of smell is keenest. What you eat affects not only the way your skin smells, but also your sense of smell. Therefore, avoid scent shopping after eating anything particularly spicy, such as Chinese or Indian food, or anything that contains a lot of garlic.

The first step is to decide on what type of fragrance you prefer (see chart page 90). You are probably drawn to the same type again and again, whether you are aware of it or not. If you are unsure about which scents fall into which category, ask the salesperson to guide you.

Try various scents on your skin, as the smell from the bottle will not be representative of what the fragrance will smell like on you. For best results, only try three or four; you will get confused if you try and sample more. Put one on the inside of each wrist and each elbow. Wait 20 or 30 minutes before deciding, as scent needs time to interact with your body chemistry. If you can, let the scent set for a few hours before choosing.

Once you have decided, buy only a small amount and try it for a few days to make sure you are happy with your decision.

There are many different strengths and formulations of scent including soaps, talcs body creams and bath oils (right).

Wearing scent

The true fragrance of scent will develop best on pulse points, where blood vessels are close to the skin surface and your body temperature is highest. These points are found on the inside of the wrists, crooks of elbows and knees, nape of the neck and between the breasts. It is a good idea to put on perfume immediately after your bath or shower, while your skin is still warm. Apply the scent using the stopper of the bottle; if it comes into contact with your fingers your body oils can alter the smell. Avoid getting scent on your clothes or jewellery. The oils in the fragrance may damage or stain the fabric or materials.

Storing scent

Exposing scent to air, heat, light and moisture causes it to lose its true smell, darken and deteriorate. Keep fragrance in a cool, dark place, and always keep the bottles tightly closed. And although large bottles sometimes seem like a good bargain, they can go bad if kept for too long. Buy fragrance in smaller containers, replacing it as you use it up.

TYPES OF SCENT	
Family	**Characteristic**
Simple floral	These scents smell like one specific flower, such as rose, lily of the valley or tuberose.
Floral bouquet	These scents are made up of elaborate combinations of several flower fragrances, in particular rose and jasmine.
Fruity	These are blended scents of orange, lemon and sometimes peach.
Chypre notes	Distinct, warm and long lasting scents based on a blend of oakmoss, amber and bergamot.
Green	These are aggressive scents, with a base smell of freshly cut grass, that are fresh and clean.
Oriental	Sensuous, with rather heavy characteristics, these scents are an intense mixture of musks and florals.
Modern blend	These scents are a complex combination of florals and spices.

MAKING UP

The right cosmetics applied correctly can add the finishing touches to your looks. You don't need a lot of expensive makeup in a variety of colours to bring out the best in your face; a few well chosen ones for different occasions and the right equipment to apply them will serve you much better. You can use makeup to achieve a natural look and enhance your facial features, and you can camouflage any facial flaws you are unhappy with. Learning to use cosmetics correctly takes some time; you need to practice to achieve the look you want.

If you have sensitive skin or are prone to allergic reactions, look for cosmetics that are hypoallergenic to reduce the chances of a reaction occurring. Never use anyone else's makeup, especially eye makeup and lipsticks. Make sure that your fingers and hands are clean before applying cosmetics, and wash your sponges, brushes and applicators regularly. Since heat, light and moisture can all damage cosmetics, it is best to store them in a drawer or cosmetic bag. It also means they are in one place when you need them.

Makeup equipment
Using the right equipment will ensure that your makeup looks as professional as it can. You should have:

- Contour brushes to apply powder, blushers and shaders.
- Eye shadow brushes or sponge-tipped applicators for powdered shadows. You will need one for each colour of shadow.
- Lip brushes, which have a chisled end, are the most accurate tool for applying lip colour.
- An eyebrow brush to train brows and to brush off excess powder.
- Sponges, either natural or synthetic, to apply liquid foundation.
- Powder puffs for applying both loose and compressed face powder.
- Cotton wool balls or cotton swabs, for blending colours and shadows.
  You should also have on hand eyebrow tweezers, eyelash curlers, and cosmetic pencil sharpeners.

THE BASIC MAKEUP

During the day you will probably want a natural look, and the colours and type of makeup you choose should reflect this. Your basic makeup will probably include foundation and powder, blush, eye shadow and mascara and lipcolour. For night you can use stronger, more vibrant colours that will look more dramatic. You may also want to use frosted or shimmery eye shadow or lip colour, apply a heavier amount of eye pencil or liner, or use a coloured mascara such as rich blue or violet.

After cleansing and moisturizing your face, the first step in doing your makeup is to apply foundation. This provides a base for the rest of your makeup, and also helps protect the skin. A highlighting cream to cover spots or shade away dark skin under the eyes is applied next. Then apply powder to help set the foundation. Blush comes next, to emphasize the cheeks. When applying eye makeup, eye shadow goes first, then eyeliner or pencil, and finally mascara. Lip colour should be applied last, as the colour and depth of your lips depends very much on the other colours you have chosen and how dramatic your eye makeup is. Often, heavily made up eyes look terrific with a light shade of lip colour, while if you are going for a more natural look in eye makeup, you can wear a richer, deeper shade of lip colour.

USING FOUNDATION

Natural looking makeup starts with the right foundation to even out skin tone and hide blemishes. The colour of your foundation should match the natural colour of your skin as closely as possible. To get an accurate match, always test the foundation on your face in natural light rather than the back of your hand. If you are unsure about the colour you should choose, ask the salesperson at the cosmetics counter for advice.

There are several types of foundation. Liquid foundation, which comes in bottles or jars, gives a light coverage and is the easiest to use. Cream foundations, which usually come in tubes or sticks, are best for skin that is blemished or very uneven in tone, since they are much thicker. You can use foundation to conceal small blemishes, but if you have scars or birthmarks, use concealing creams designed for the purpose.

Applying foundation

Your face should be cleansed and moisturized before applying foundation. Place a small amount of foundation on the back of your hand. Using clean fingertips or a dampened sponge, apply the foundation in even strokes to one side of the face at a time. Start with the forehead and spread it with circular strokes to ensure even application. Work it right up to the hairline, avoiding any harsh lines. Work down from the temple, over the cheek, and under the eye. Repeat for the other side. Place a dab of foundation on each side of the nose, blending carefully up over the nose and the eyelids. Then cover your chin, lips and jawline, blending in the foundation carefully. Remove any surplus foundation on the neck, then blot all over the face with a tissue.

If you have small spots or dark circles under the eye you want to hide, a highlighting cream can be used. Choose a colour only one shade lighter than your own skin tone for the most natural look. You will get the best results if you use a flat brush to apply the cream into the hollows of the shadow and then gradually blend it into the rest of your makeup.

Cosmetic basics include foundation, powder, blush, eye makeup and lip colour and are available for every skin colour and tone (overleaf).

USING POWDER

Powder is essential to help set your foundation and provide a grease-free surface for the rest of your makeup. It gives a natural finish to your skin and helps stop an oily shine from developing.

Powder is available both loose and compressed. Loose powder provides a translucent, natural-looking matte finish. It is more successful at setting foundation, and keeps the colour of powder eye shadows and blushes strong. Compressed powder is best used for touchups during the day. Because it contains a binding agent, pressed powder goes on heavier than loose. It also has a tendency to streak. Choose a powder that matches your natural skin tone or, to add a warmer glow, pick one that is pink or peach tinted. With pressed powder, you may want to choose a shade that is lighter than your skin tone to compensate for any colour build up.

Applying powder

For loose powder you should use a large soft makeup brush to dust it on all over your face, including the eyelids. Don't rub the powder into the skin. Remove any surplus by using the brush to stroke downwards. Be sure and remove any loose powder around the brows and the jaw and neck. With pressed powder, use the puff or brush in short, downward strokes that follow the direction of the facial hair.

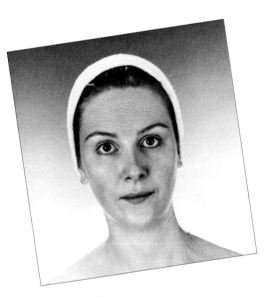

When applying foundation, work on one side of the face at a time. Start at the forehead and cover the entire area up to the hairline.

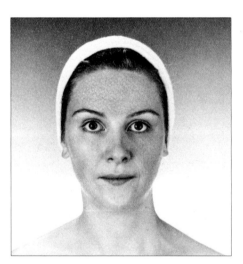

Work foundation down from the temple over the cheek and under the eye area. Blend well to avoid any harsh lines, then repeat for other side.

USING BLUSH

Applied correctly, blush can light up your face and add a strong healthy glow to the skin. When you use blush it should look as if you have just blushed for real, or have a little colour in your cheeks.

Blush comes in cream, stick and powder form; the pressed powder ones are the easiest to use. The colour you choose depends on your skin tone and hair colouring. A sheer, matte colour looks the most natural, and using less is always better than using more. Don't use the glittery or shimmering blushes during the day. Save these for an evening look.

Applying blush

For most women blush should be applied in the "pork chop" shape from the cheekbone to the outer corner of the eyebrow. Feel for the top of your cheekbone beneath the middle of the eye; you should apply blush from that point up along the cheekbone and finish with a light curve of colour near the tip of your eyebrow. If you have a very round face you might want to apply blush slightly lower on your cheeks or wherever colour occurs naturally.

For best results with powder blush, apply after foundation and powder. Run your brush lightly over the blush compact, blow on the bristles to remove excess colour, and brush on blush a with a quick, crescent-shaped stroke. Clean your brush on a tissue, then bend blush with short feathery strokes.

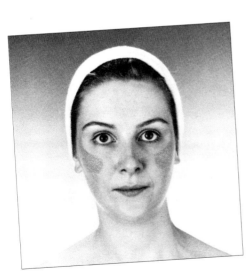

Apply blush starting on the cheekbone below the outer corner of the eye and work your way to the tip of your eyebrow up towards the hairline. Be sure and blend well.

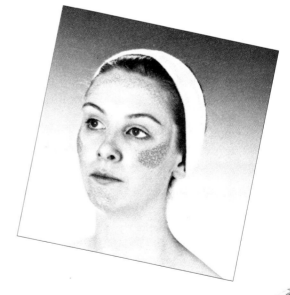

For a healthy glow apply blush to your forehead, temples and chin. Use lightly and blend it towards the hairline or the jawline.

USING EYE MAKEUP

Your eyes are the feature that you are likely to want to emphasize, and eye makeup is probably the one area that you will want to experiment with different colours, shading, and types. Eye makeup should be applied skilfully and professionally if you are to get the look you want.

Applying eye shadow

The first step is to pick the colours that best suit you. Eye shadow colours should flatter your eye colour without matching it, as this can look too harsh. Neither must they match the colour of your clothing. The easiest type of shadow to use and the type that has the widest variety of colours, is pressed powder.

The key to applying shadow is to blend it well so there are no harsh edges. Using a neutral colour, work from the inner to the outer corner of the eye. To define the shape of the socket use a shadow a shade or two darker than the first and apply this slightly above the crease in the socket and down to the top of the lid. Use a lighter shade under the browbone to highlight the eyes. Blend the shadows well, using your fingertips or a cotton swab.

Applying liner

Eyelining can be used to accentuate the shape of the eyes. Most liners are now in pencil form, although some are in liquid or in cake form that you add water to. If you use a pencil make sure that it is soft enough not to drag the skin as you use it. To apply, simply line the upper lid close to the lashes, and the lower lid below the lashes. You should use a colour similar to your shadow, and blend it with your fingertip or a cotton swab to avoid harsh lines.

Applying mascara

There are so many different formulas of mascara on the market it is really just a matter of choice as to the one you use. To apply mascara, use several thin coats to avoid the lashes sticking together. Coat the inside of the top lashes first, then the inside of the bottom lashes. Brush them using an eyelash brush, allow mascara to dry, then apply another coat if necessary.

Eyebrows

If you have thick or unruly eyebrows, you may want to tweeze them to get a better shape. Always work with the natural shape of the brow, and never remove hair from above the brow; only remove the stragglers below.

If you feel your eyebrows need defining, use a light eyebrow pencil that blends in with the colour and tone of your hair and brows. Brush your brows to eliminate any loose foundation or powder. Start at the inner corner of the eyebrow and apply short, light, upward strokes of the pencil as you work towards the middle. From the centre of the eyebrow to the outer edge, use the same kind of strokes as before but this time tip them downwards.

For prominent eyes, use a matte eye shadow in a muted shade over the entire lid up to browbone. Avoid frosted or dark shadows, which emphasize the shape. Apply a matte highlighter over the darker shadow on the browbone. Use eyeliner on both lids and blend away the hard edges on the top lid. Then apply lots of mascara.

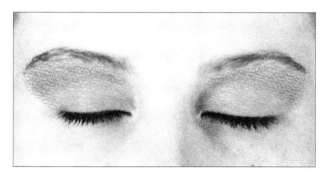

Deep set eyes can be enhanced by ensuring that the eyebrows are neat and tidy and not too heavy. Use a pale shadow on the lid in either powder or pencil form, and a darker shadow on the browbone. Do not use too heavy or dark a shadow because this make the eyes appear even further set back.

For wide set eyes you should accentuate the inner corner. Starting close to the nose, use a darker shadow to cover the inner half of the eye. Use a lighter shade for the outer half but do not extend it past the corner of the eye. Highlight the browbone and use eyeliner on both upper and lower lids.

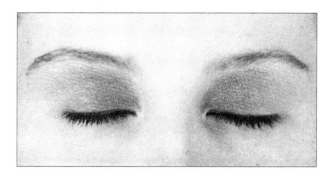

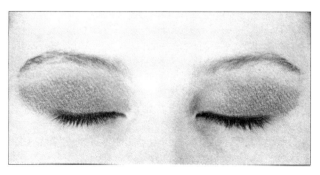

Close set eyes need emphasis at the outer corners. Cover the lid with shadow going beyond the outer corners. Apply paler shadow to the inner corner above the socket and on the lid. Apply highlighter on the browbone and line the both lids from the centre out. Apply mascara to outer lashes only.

MAKING UP

USING LIP COLOUR

Lip colour is the finishing touch to your makeup, and the right colour can make all the difference. There is a wide variety of shades available, from the sheerest of glosses to the richest of reds. Your lip colour should complement your skin tone, not the clothes you wear. If your skin has a yellowish cast, choose lip colours in the apricot, peach and brown families. If your skin has a bluish undertone, go for pinks and bluish reds. If teeth are yellowed go for pink, red, plum, or mauve lip colours.

If you have very full lips, avoid shiny or pastel shades, both of which draw attention to lip size and shape; use muted colours instead. For small lips, avoid dark colours; use brighter colours to make your mouth look larger and fuller. To tone down dark lips, apply foundation, blot it with a tissue and then allow it to dry before applying colour.

Applying lip colour

To get great looking lips you should use a lip pencil for lining and a lipbrush to apply colour. To achieve the most natural line, sharpen the pencil for every use, then rub the tip down with a tissue to blunt the point slightly. Start at the bow of your mouth (the top centre), then line one side of the upper lip. Line the other side, then do the bottom lip in one smooth curve. Use a good lipbrush to soften the pencil line, smoothing out any harsh edges.

Work some lip colour on to the lipbrush and fill in the line from the centre of the mouth to the corners. Work gradually towards the line but don't cover it with lipstick. Open your mouth wide and apply lipstick in the corners of your mouth. Blot off the excess with a tissue to hold the colour and prevent smearing.

You can change your lip shape with the correct application of lip colour. For thin lips, apply foundation over the entire lip and mouth area and line with a lip pencil just outside the natural line of your lips. Fill this in with your

For perfect lips you should always use a lip pencil and outline your lips. Choose one that matches your lip colour.

Use a lipbrush to fill in the outline with colour. Blot off any excess lip colour with a paper tissue to prevent smearing.

chosen lip colour. Use a bright shade or a rich gloss to make lips appear fuller. To play down full lips, apply foundation and then pencil a line just inside the natural lip line. Apply your colour inside this line but avoid glosses or very bright colours, and blot off any extra sheen.

MAKEUP FOR BLONDES

There are various shades of blonde, from platinum to mousy, and makeup colours will need to be reflect this.

Pale blondes tend to have a pale translucent complexion and light coloured eyes. It is important to try and maintain a natural look with makeup, and light shades should be used. Choose colours wisely, as pale blondes can look washed out if the colours are too mild. Use foundations with a hint of rose, and keep to the same family for blushers to bring out a rosy glow. Pale blondes usually have very light coloured eyes, so shadows should not be too dark. Grey, taupe, teal and mauve should look terrific with pale skin and light eyes. A rose colour is also necessary for the lips; pink gloss, dusty rose, and pinks with a hint of plum should all complement your colouring.

Natural blondes often have a lot of red in their hair, so they can take stronger colours. Smoky colours, such as plum, grey and green, look good around the eyes. Choose pink to plum blushers, and pink or red lip colours.

Golden blondes often have skin with more orange and brown tones in it. Their skin is often uneven in colour and may need toning down. Keep the foundation ivory to beige, and use warm peachy tones for makeup. Try peach or coral blushers, while for eyes you can wear all shades of brown, such as rich russet, any shadow with golden tones, and even smoky blues to violets. Lip colours should also echo the peachy tones of your skin. Try peach, coral, browns such as mocha, and an orange red colour.

MAKEUP FOR BRUNETTES

Brunettes, too, vary in skin colour. Their complexions range from pale white-beige with a hint of pink, to light or dark olive skin.

For brunettes with light skin, foundation should have a hint of beige in it; avoid any with gold tones. Blusher should always include a rosy glow; try a pink with a hint of blue, rose brown or rose wine. Brunettes usually have brown or hazel eyes. To bring out the colour, use plums, taupes, grey or green eye shadows; some of these will make brown eyes look darker, while others will make them look lighter. Light-skinned brunettes can look very dramatic with rich coloured lips. Try a true red, a pink-plum, or a burgundy shade.

Olive-skinned brunettes often have very uneven skin colour. You may need a concealer to even out the blotchy patches. Earth tones are usually the

best for this type of skin; the darker your skin the more dramatic the colour can be. Paler skins should stick to a softer look. Try green, bronze, or brown around the eyes and highlight with a creamy gold.

Dark-skinned brunettes usually have a natural bloom and even skin colouring, so little foundation is necessary. A bronzing gel may be the answer if a little coverage or colour is desired. Blushers in brick or wine shades are the most flattering; try to avoid blushes with too much pink or red in them. Eye shadows to try include the green through copper shades, golden brown and bronze colours. Lips, too, should echo the earthy tones of the skin. Try plums, wines and various shades of brown.

MAKEUP FOR REDHEADS

Redheads are known for their fair, delicate and often freckled skin. The hair colour can range from light red to a dark auburn. Keep foundation light, so as to not cover up or hide freckles. Golden beige or creamy beige shades are suitable. You should stick to natural colours for cheeks and lips. In blushers, again the rich peach and apricot shades will best suit you. Eye shadow colours that will complement your colouring include greens, russets, rust, teal and golden copper. The lips should continue the peach palette, so try brick red, corals or peaches.

MAKEUP FOR BLACKS

Black skins have an incredible variety of skin tones, and no one makeup colour will be perfect for them all. There are specific makeup ranges that have been developed for black skins; not only to accomodate the different texture of black skin, but also to cater for the range of skin colours. In general, stay away from the muddy colours and try the clear vivid ones that often look harsh on pale complexions.

Black skin tends to be oily but with small pores, so oil-based foundations may not adhere well to the skin. If your skin is yellow or ashy in tone, try adding a pink tinted moisturizer to your foundation. Use a pinky blush to bring out your skin's natural glow. Black skin is also often patchy and uneven in tone, and dark circles under the eyes may need to be camouflaged. Use a camouflage stick in a lighter shade than your foundation and choose a shadow with an earthy tone, such as brown, burgundy, beige, or copper.

Black-skinned women can often wear the shiny, iridescent eye shadows that paler women cannot. Try some of the brighter shades such as emerald green or peacock blue, the metallics like gold, silver or copper, and even the fun shades like neon pink, sunshine yellow or orange.

Lip colour is often uneven, with the upper lip being darker than the lower. Use a dark base on the lighter lip or try a lip corrector. Opt for a matte-finish lipstick rather than a lip gloss, as it will help hide lip problems better.

Nighttime makeup includes iridescent glittery eye shadows and pearlized lipsticks in fun vivid colours (right).

NIGHTTIME MAKEUP

For a special nighttime look, you will probably want to wear more makeup than you do during the day. This means applying more blusher, using eye pencil or eye liner, and possibly even wearing false eyelashes. In addition, the colours you choose should be brighter, richer and clearer than those for a daytime look. Go for the dramatic cosmetics such as royal blue, violet or emerald green mascara, and wear metallic iridescent eye shadows that will reflect the light. Blush can also be iridescent. Lips, too, should stand out at night, so pick pearlized colours in rich clear shades.

CHANGING MAKEUP WITH AGE

As you get older you will probably need to change the colours of your cosmetics. Bright rich colours can draw attention to older skin and show up wrinkles, lines and bags. And as your hair colour usually changes as you get older, your makeup should reflect this. Try experimenting with new colours and products, and try out new ways of applying your makeup. Avoid any makeup with a shimmery pearlized effect, as this accentuates the skin creases.

Because older skin is drier, you may need a lighter textured foundation. Always use plenty of moisturizer before applying. Your skin colour may also fade with age and the colour of your foundation may need to be changed. Use a minimum of powder, as it can dry in the wrinkles and crevices of older skin. Avoid complicated shading and highlighting, as these can look unnatural on wrinkled skin; keep your makeup simple.

The area around the eyes is the area that wrinkles most easily and tends to show age first. Stick to neutral coloured shadows; don't use frosted colours or highlighters, as these draw attention to wrinkles. Avoid using cream shadows, which can crease easily. Use bright colours carefully. Use an eye pencil with a light hand, as you can easily pull the delicate skin around this area, and avoid heavy lining of the eyes.

Your eyebrows and lashes tend to become more sparse as you get older, so you may need to use eyebrow pencil and a different formula of mascara than you did previously. Try false eyelashes, to add thickness to your natural lashes. You may also want to experiment with applying individual lashes to supplement your own.

As you age, the natural lip line becomes less well defined. This is complicated by wrinkle lines running into the lip shape, which can cause lip colour to bleed. To avoid this, apply foundation and powder before lip colour, and always use a lip brush to apply colour. Avoid lip gloss, and choose your colours carefully. If lip colour is too pale it will look washed out, but if it is too bright it will look garish and more ageing. Also, avoid pearlized or shimmery lip colours, which can also look ageing.

MAKING UP

CAMOUFLAGING FACIAL FAULTS

Facial faults can easily be corrected with makeup if you have a steady hand and the right equipment. All it takes is a little practice and the clever use of contourers. You should have a selection of concealers and some sponges cut into wedges available to apply concealers. Study your face when it is clean and makeup free to see what areas you would like to disguise. Make sure the light is bright, and experiment with different techniques. Study the effect from different angles to make sure the look is the one you want.

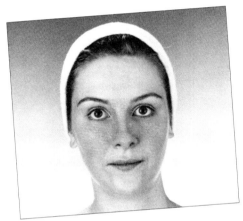

To slim down a wide nose, run a line of darker foundation down the length of the nose on either side. Blend lightly, then apply lighter foundation down the centre.

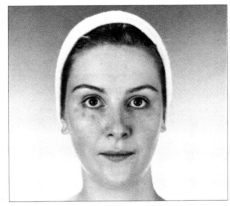

Dark circles under the eyes can easily be disguised with pale concealer. Dot it lightly under the eyes towards the cheekbones and blend well with the fingers or a brush.

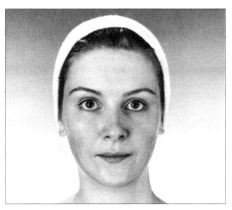

To soften a heavy jaw, use a darker shade of foundation along the jawline down the sides of the jaw below the ears and blend well.

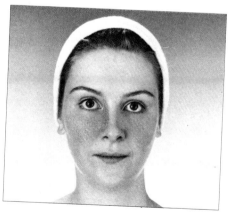

To make a crooked nose appear smooth and straight, use a darker foundation or a contouring stick on the side that juts out and a pale colour on the opposite side.

COSMETIC SURGERY

If you have facial faults that you seriously feel uncomfortable with, and ones that cannot be corrected by makeup, cosmetic surgery may provide the answer. It can be used to correct a number of faults, both large and small. It is often used to remove some of the signs of ageing, or to improve the balance of facial features.

Before you decide to have cosmetic surgery, it is important that you are realistic about what cosmetic surgery can and cannot do. Discuss your feelings with your doctor, who will be able to recommend a reputable plastic surgeon. And listen to his or her advice about what surgery will be able to accomplish. It is no good asking for a small button nose if it won't fit with your other features. The doctor should also tell you how long the procedure takes, what the after-effects are, and how long it takes before your new features have settled in.

Types of surgery

Rhinoplasty, which is altering the shape of the nose, is one of the most common surgical procedures. Almost any shape of nose can be made bigger or smaller, and bumps can easily be removed. The miminum age for surgery is about 18 years old, when the facial features have stopped growing. All the surgical work is carried out inside the nose, so there is no visible scarring. Only a brief stay in hospital is necessary, although the swelling and bruising around the nose and eyes lasts for about two to three weeks after surgery. It takes about six months for the nose to assume its new shape.

Blepharoplasty is the procedure to remove bags under the eyes and to correct drooping upper lids. The procedure is simple and the scarring can easily be hidden by clever use of makeup.

Prominent or protruding ears are pinned back in a procedure called otoplasty. As the incision is made behind the ears, the scarring is not visible and results of the procedure are excellent.

Cosmetic surgery can also reduce or augment a chin, making it seem more in line with the rest of the face. These procedures are more complicated than some, and there may be visible scarring, but the results are usually excellent.

A face lift is a common procedure. It is a complicated and fairly lengthy operation, as several areas of the face have to be treated. In this the skin is actually lifted up the forehead and tightened back by the ears; if it is not done correctly you can look and feel worse than you did before the operation. Small scars usually remain behind the ears and at the hairline, but these can easily be concealed. The effect of a face lift lasts from about two to five years, depending on the woman. After this time the skin starts to sag again and show signs of ageing. You can have more than one face lift if the effects are not as long lasting as you would like. Many women have more than one operation during their lifetime.

DRESS SENSE

One of the quickest ways to change your look is to change the way you dress. In addition, the way you dress and present yourself is a good indication of the kind of impression you are trying to make.

Having the right clothes for different occasions is also important, as you dress differently for the various times in your life. If you learn to dress to suit your colouring, figure and lifestyle you will be more confident and comfortable with yourself and you will present an attractive image to those who see you.

USING COLOUR

It is no secret that colour plays an important part in our lives, and the colour of your clothes can make a tremendous difference in how attractive you appear. When you have bought a new outfit in a colour that really suits you, you will notice it and other people will too. Colour is one of the most important ways of enhancing your look; the wrong colour, however, can detract from it.

When choosing your wardrobe, it is best to start with a few neutral colours that suit you and then build around them. The most versatile neutral base colours include navy, grey, black and beige. You can then add additional colours that are the most flattering to you, and know that most of the pieces in your wardrobe can work together to create a look that is your own.

Finding your colours

The colours best suited to you usually depend on your hair and skin tone, just as it does with your makeup colours. It is worth going shopping and trying on clothes in various colours that you were hesitant to try before, to see if they suit you or not. Invest the time and effort to experiment a little and get a good idea of what works for you. Some of the colours will make you look vibrant and alive, while in others you may appear washed out and drab. Most people can wear most colours, it is the shade and intensity of the colour that determines whether it will work for them.

Although instinct is often better than going by the book, there are some guidelines you can follow when choosing colours. Light-skinned brunettes look best in clear, stark colours, such as black, white, red and blue, but should avoid warm colours with a lot of gold and yellow. They should also stay away from the baby soft pastels, which can look dull and drab. Dark-skinned brunettes or black women can wear the same range of colours as light skinned brunettes, but can go for the bolder colours such as bright blue and hot pink, which often bring out the rich amber tones of their complexions.

Blondes look best in a different range of colours, especially the soft blues and pinks. Neutrals, like off-white and camel also flatter pale skinned blondes. Golden-skinned blondes should wear colours that emphasize their tawny looks, such as golds, yellows and corals. Other warm colours, like cream, peach and ivory are also flattering.

Redheads look best in colours that are rich and lush, such as green, oranges and olives. Other good colours for redheads include cinnamon, salmon and brick red. Pinks and plum shades are not suitable for most redheads, and very bright colours should be avoided as they can overwhelm the hair colour.

It is important to reassess your colours on a regular basis, especially if you change your hair colour. Also, as colouring changes with age, you may find that as you get older your favourite colours are no longer the most flattering, while others that you once dismissed now suit you perfectly.

USING COLOUR
The photograph overleaf shows a selection of colours that flatter blondes, brunettes, redheads and blacks. Blacks (1) can easily wear rich, vibrant colours as can brunettes (2). Blondes (3) look good in pastels, as well as lighter tones of the colours that brunettes can easily wear. Redheads (4) look best in earthy colours, such as brown, peach, coral and green, which flatter their skin and hair colour.

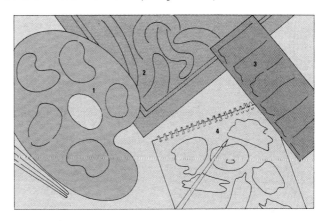

DRESS FOR YOUR SHAPE

It is not only the colour of your clothes that makes a difference to your look, but the right shape will flatter your figure no end. Although most women want to look fashionable, it is important not to dress in styles just because they are popular if they are unsuitable for you. Instead of looking stylish, you may just look silly. There are lots of tricks to hide a thick waistline or short legs, for instance, if you know what your body shape is and how to dress for it. Once you recognize which styles, fabrics and shapes suit you, you can emphasize your good points, and disguise your bad.

Determining your shape
Almost all figure faults can be camouflaged or disguised with the right clothes. The main factors to consider when deciding your shape include height (tall or short), weight (thin or heavy), and your overall body shape. The most common shapes are rounded all over; straight up and down, with little hip or bust definition; pear shaped, with its small shoulders and wide hips; or top heavy, with big shoulders or busts and smaller hips.

Dressing for your shape

Most women know that vertical stripes make you look taller and thinner, while horizontal stripes are widening. But it isn't just the pattern of the fabric that affects whether a garment will look good on you. The overall shape, the waistline, and neckline, will all determine whether it suits you or not. It is important to take all of these into consideration when you are shopping for a new outfit.

Tall women

Tall women need to wear clothes that detract from their height rather than elongate their look. To do this you should:

- Avoid tiny prints or patterns, which will just get lost on you. Larger prints and more vibrant colours will suit you well.
- You can wear heavier textures, such as tweed and bulky mohairs, without getting lost in the clothes.
- Avoid vertical stripes, which elongate the body; stick to horizontals if you are slender.
- When buying skirts, avoid those that are long and straight, which will make you look taller and accentuate your height; wear them just below the knee or even shorter. You should also choose flared or wide skirts to provide width.
- Instead of a monochromatic look, wear different coloured layers to break up the line of the body and add breadth.
- Pleated trousers or trousers with wide legs will minimize your height.
- A wide contrast-colour belt breaks up the lines of the body and divides it into more equal proportions.

Short women

Tiny and petite women need to dress tall and should choose clothes that do not make them look doll-like. You should:

- Avoid large prints and designs, which will overpower you. Also, avoid horizontal stripes, which can make you look tiny and wide. Choose vertical stripes and prints instead to add height.
- Outfits with wide belts cut the body in half; wear same-coloured belts or none at all.
- Sweaters cropped at the waist and short jackets can look terrific and add length and height.
- Clothes should be simple and uncluttered; avoid exaggerated details patch pockets or full lapels on jackets.
- Your skirts should always look longer than they do wide. Straight, A-line and tiny pleated skirts are flattering; avoid the very full dirndl skirts, which can balloon out on a small woman.
- A monochromatic colour scheme lengthens the body; don't break up the body with contrasting coloured belts.

DRESS SENSE

Heavy women

Heavy, rounded women can look even larger if they are wearing the wrong clothes. You should:

- Invest in some good quality shapely bras, including a strapless one.
- Avoid horizontal stripes, which will make you look wider. Also, avoid fabrics with large designs or prints for the same reason.
- Don't wear gathered skirts, or shirts and dresses with patch pockets at the hips, which will emphasize your width.
- Don't wear clinging fabrics or bulky, long haired furs, which add width to your figure.
- The most flattering neck shape is the V-neck, which elongates the neck and lengthens the torso.
- Choose outfits in one colour scheme to add length and height to your body.
- Don't try and hide a thick waist with blousy garments. If you are short or thick waisted, choose dresses that have a belt made of the same fabric or wear none at all.

Thin women

Women who are very slender need to find clothes that will widen their look. You should:

- Avoid clinging fabrics, which will emphasize your thin figure.
- Wear round or crew necklines, as the V-neck will add length to a thin neck.
- Choose fabrics with horizontal stripes, plaids and patterns to add some bulk and width to the figure.
- Avoid long fitted clothes, which add length to your look.
- Clothes with design features, such as double breasted suit jackets, skirts with large patch pockets, and pleated trousers can all look flattering.
- Blouses with yokes and ruffles add shape and width.

Top heavy women

Women who are busty or have broad shoulders need clothes that distract the eye from the top half of the body and that balance out the dimensions of their hips and bust.

- Avoid blousy and full sweaters and blouses, which emphasize the bust.
- V necks are the most flattering, as they elongate the line of the neck. Large shoulder pads, too, may help balance out a large bust.
- With a shapely bust a low neckline in the evening can be a terrific morale booster.
- The long lean sweater that is hip length or longer can stretch out a rounded figure and help disguise a big bust.
- Dropped waists are stylish, but if you are heavy with a large bust you can look large and boxy.
- Avoid high waistlines, which can emphasize a large bust.

DRESS SENSE

DRESSING FOR YOUR SHAPE

The right clothes can make all the difference to how you feel about yourself and can influence how other people see you. When you feel that you look good you are more confident and sure of yourself and others will respond to this attitude. Few women are completely satisfied with their body shape.

Heavy women should wear darker colours to look slimmer. The longer skirt adds to the height to create a slimmer look. The V-neck is good as it adds length to the torso, making it look longer and slimmer.

Thin women need to choose clothes that add bulk and width. The textured sweater and big collar provide a wider look for the shoulders, while the light colours of the outfit provide a larger but softer effect.

Bottom heavy women need clothes that balance out the top and bottom halves of their bodies. The blouse with a tie and shoulder pads add width to shoulders and bust, making them seem more in proportion with the hips.

Although there is little you can do to change your basic body shape, there are lots of tricks you can use to successfully disguise any figure faults you feel you have. The women shown here all fit into one of the categories of basic figure types and have dressed correctly to suit their shape. The clothes they are wearing are suitable for them and help to disguise their figure flaws.

Top heavy women also need to balance out the two halves of their bodies. Here, the detail on the shoulder brings the eye up and helps to balance out a larger bust and the soft draping effect of the overblouse is flattering.

Short women who are also petite need clothes that do not overpower them. The one-piece straight dress helps to elongate the line of the body. Wearing stockings and shoes in the same colour helps to accentuate the vertical line.

Tall women need clothes that detract from their height. This layered look adds breadth and the wide belt divides the body into more equal proportions. The tucks in the skirt add fullness, and a skirt that ends just below the knees helps to cut long legs.

Bottom heavy women

The bottom heavy woman, often called pear-shaped, is the most common figure type; it is also the easiest to disguise. You should:

- Avoid tops that end at your widest point, which is usually around the hips, or horizontal stripes that hit you around the hips or bottom.
- When choosing trousers, those with a pleated waistline will help smooth figures that are wide at the hips.
- Avoid very short skirts, which will make thick legs and thighs look stumpy.
- Wide cinch belts will emphasize a tiny waist, but will make hips and bottom look enormous.
- Choose blouses and jackets with bust or shoulder detail to draw the eye upwards. Shoulder pads may also help balance the look.

USING ACCESSORIES

It is not only the clothes you wear but what you wear them with that tells the true story. Accessories can change an entire outfit, disguise figure flaws, take a dress from day to night or update last year's favourite to be this year's model. It is smart to have a good selection of accessories, such as jewellery, bags and belts, scarves, and hats, to add some punch to your outfits and extend your wardrobe.

Although accessories do not have to cost a lot to look good, it is wise to invest in a few classics. This may include some good pieces of jewellery, one or two good leather bags and belts, a few scarves or shawls, and a selection of well-fitting shoes. Choose styles and colours that can be worn with a wide variety of outfits in your wardrobe. This way the initial investment will not seem so great as you can wear them with almost everything.

In addition, make sure that you have a selection of inexpensive fun pieces that can be worn with your more casual clothes. This may include plastic or metal jewellery in bright colours, rubber or fake leopard print belts or scarves, and some fabric shoes.

The ethnic look is always popular, and these accessories are usually made out of natural fabrics, such as leather, cotton, or linen. Ethnic jewellery is usually out of clay, seashells, beads, feathers or wood. They look terrific with batik-printed cotton skirts and tops.

Jewellery

There is such a wide range of jewellery available today in so many different styles that you can change your look almost every day. Some is suitable for daywear, while other pieces glitter and are perfect for night.

When buying jewellery, look for pieces that have distinct shapes or colours and can stand on their own to create a personal look. Jewellery doesn't have to perfectly match the colour of your clothes, or be a set to be worn together.

There are few hard and fast rules when it comes to wearing jewellery. Generally, the simpler the outfit the more dramatic the jewellery can be. It doesn't mean you need to wear a lot of jewellery, but a large bold necklace will add more to a plain black dress than a lot of dainty necklaces and bracelets. Take out all your pieces, play around with them and experiment to find out which ones work together; you may be surprised.

Brooches are one of the most versatile pieces of jewellery you can have. They can be worn in a variety of ways to add sparkle to an outfit. Try using them on hats, on belts, or to hold scarves and shawls together.

When choosing earrings, your hair may determine which styles look best on you. If you have very short hair or wear your hair up, you can take large bold earrings, which will just get lost in layered shaggy manes; also, large dangling earrings may get tangled in long hair. For a professional look, wear small buttons or studs. Blondes and redheads look good in gold tones, while darker hair takes to silver and chrome.

Scarves

Scarves are one of the best wardrobe updates around, especially when you wear them in an unexpected way. Scarves can be used to introduce colour, provide a contrast and create shape in an outfit.

When buying scarves colour is important, but there is no need to be overly cautious. Don't be afraid to mix brights with brights, and pastel shades look terrific against black and neutral tones. Prints can work with prints, but when mixing be sure that at least one of the colours is similar. Don't pass over a print because it looks exaggerated in the store; the effect will be muted when rolled and wrapped around the neck.

You can wear scarves in a number of different ways. Wrapping them around the head can look terrific, although getting the look right may take some practice. They can also be worn tied loosely around the neck or wrapped around the waist as a belt.

Belts

Belts are an important fashion accessory and can change a look completely. The choice today is enormous, and the right belt can make or break an outfit. Belts can also help disguise certain figure flaws that you may have. Bright colours draw attention, so if your waist is wide stick to neutral colours, which are more slimming. Belts slung low on the hips can lengthen the torso and make you look thinner, and thick waists look best in thin belts.

Leather belts are not your only option, and it is worth investigating some of the others. Try a fake leopard skin, suede, or rubber belt for a different look. And look for belts that have interesting or unusual buckles. You may be able to find antique buckles in markets or stalls that you can put on your favourite belt. For nighttime, look for jewelled, glittery belts that can add sparkle to an evening look.

Accessories such as bags and belts, jewellery and hats come in different materials and add the finishing touches to your look (overleaf).

DRESS SENSE

CHANGING YOUR LOOK

You can use accessories to dramatically change your look. You can go from day to night, from city to country, or from casual to glamorous, all with a few simple accessories. Pay attention to your bags and shoes, the colours and textures that you choose, and add a few pieces of well-chosen jewellery . Take a simple black dress and see what you can do.

For a country-style look, keep to warm, earthy colours. Wear low heeled leather shoes, a simple leather belt and carry a casual leather bag. Wrap a patterned shawl over your shoulders and tuck the ends into your belt or secure it at the neck with a brooch.

Keep to simple accessories in one colour for a dressy daytime look. The hat, belt, bag and stockings are all in a sharp, bright red, which contrasts beautifully with the black. Jewellery should be kept to a minimum. If wearing red shoes instead of black, change your stockings to blend in with the colour of the dress.

Go for broke when dressing up at night. Evening accessories are best in the metallics, such as gold or silver. Wrap a shimmery fringed shawl around your shoulders and wear a fake leopard skin hat to add a touch of class. At night, legwear such as stockings or tights should always be as sheer as possible, and shoes and gloves should be in sophisticated materials such as leather or patent. With jewellery, wear a few well-chosen bold dramatic pieces rather than a lot of small dainty ones — the impact you make will be that much greater. Keep to jewellery in metallics, and make sure your earrings are big enough to be seen and make a statement.

For a fun daytime look, take some tips from the fashions of the fifties. Wrap a colourful scarf around your head, cross it in front and tie it at the side of your neck. Then put on a man's black felt hat, Italian movie-star style. Pick out the brightest colour in the scarf, in this case blue, and wear a belt and stockings to match. Wear long fake leather gloves and high-heeled stiletto shoes. Wear a small black leather bag with the strap running from one shoulder across your chest so the bag sits on the opposite hip. A simple silver bangle and silver beaded necklace completes the look.

Hats

Although most women don't wear hats every day, we all have occasions in which a hat is called for. The most important factor when choosing a hat is whether it suits your face shape (see page 51). You need to get the balance right so that the hat looks as if it is part of your outfit and not an afterthought.

A heart shaped face looks best in hats with a medium-sized brim that is worn tilted slightly. Square faces are strong boned and need balance. Tiny hats perched on top of the head don't work, so choose a wide brimmed hat worn flat to counter the strong jawline. Hats for a long face shouldn't fit too snugly, such as cloches or flat pull-on styles. The most flattering shape has curves and brim detail. Brims that curve up are also flattering. Round faces need hats that provide angles and length. Deep crowned hats worn low on the forehead are suitable, as are hats worn tilted at an angle.

When buying a hat for a special occasion, take your outfit with you. What you thought was a perfect match in the store may turn out to be a complete mistake. When choosing a style, remember that if you are going to be greeting a lot of people, in a reception line for instance, a wide brimmed hat is going to get in the way. If you will be sitting for a long time, too high a hat will make it difficult for people behind you to see.

Your hairstyle, too, is important. Few hats look good worn with lots of fringe or hair in the front. Try and find a neatly pinned-back style that is flattering, and wear your hair this way when hat shopping so you will get the real effect of the hat.

Shoes

There are not too many rules when it comes to choice of shoes, and fashions in shoes come and go. The height of the heel is an indicator of the look you are trying to achieve; flats or low heeled shoes are usually more casual or better for a professional look, while high heels are almost always only worn at night.

Since the style, cut and colour of a shoe can appear to alter the shape of your foot and ankle, it is important to follow a few rules when choosing your footwear. White and bright colours draw attention to your feet, while darker neutral colours blend in. Large or very narrow feet are emphasized by shoes with pointed toes or styles cut high over the foot. Thick ankles are not helped by very high or low heels; the medium heeled classic pump is the best shape. Small feet can take shoes that are decorated with button or bows, but small women should not wear very high heels.

The most important factor is to buy shoes that fit, to avoid foot problems developing. Try on shoes with the stockings or socks you are planning to wear them with. Always try on both shoes of a pair, as one foot is usually larger than the other. Don't buy shoes when you are hot, as your feet may be swollen and you won't get an accurate fitting. And always make sure that your shoes fit correctly across the broadest part of your feet.

INDEX

Bold type indicates main reference

CREDITS

Photography
Dave King pp 56–57, 94–95, 101, 102,
103, 104, 105, 112–113, 120–121,
122–123
Chris Knaggs pp 28–29, 32, 42–43, 46,
49, 64–65, 68, 78–79, 84–85, 89
Vidal Sassoon pp 52–53
Science Photo Library pg 39

Illustrations
Nancy Anderson pp 7, 23, 37, 62, 75,
91, 109
Kevin Molloy pp 116–117
Howard Pemberton pp 27, 34, 44, 51,
66, 72, 83, 96, 97, 99, 100, 101

ACKNOWLEDGEMENTS

We would like to thank the following for
their generosity with information and
products.

Accessories
Accessorize
Molton Brown hair accessories
Next
Additional jewellery courtesy of
Liz Wolf-Cohen
Hats by Alan White

Cosmetics
Almay
Colorfast
Laboratoires RoC (UK) Ltd.

Lancome for Les Aqua waterproof
makeup
Mary Quant
Max Factor
Prescriptives
Swedish Formula
Yves Saint Laurent
Cosmetic brushes by Stephen Glass at
Face Facts and the Cosmetic Brush
Company

Perfume
Christian Dior
Guerlain
Nina Ricci
Worth

SPECIAL THANKS TO

Boots, Crabtree and Evelyn, and the
Body Shop for the selection of toiletries
and beauty accessories; Revlon for
suggesting makeup colours for blondes,
brunettes, and redheads; Fashion Fair for
suggesting makeup colours for blacks;
Claire at Trevor Sorbie for hair colouring
pp 56–57; Mark Hayes at Vidal Sassoon
for hairstyles pp 52–53; Maxine Tobias
and Mary Stewart for photos pp. 14–15,
18, 20–21, taken from the book *Stretch
and Relax*.